Sam Gates is an author, cookery teacher and member of The Guild of Food Writers. She worked as marketing director of the UK's first food channel before starting her own company, working with clients such as BBC Food, BBC Radio and small food producers. But above all, Sam loves to cook for her family and friends, which she does at any opportunity.

Sam's first family cookbook *Food for Your Brood* was followed by the popular *The Tin & Traybake Cookbook*, published by Robinson in 2018. Juggling family, work, life and cooking was the inspiration behind her third book, Amazon bestseller *The Batch Cook Book*, which was described by the *Guardian* as 'redefining the concept of batch cooking'.

The Green Batch Cook Book is Sam's fourth book. Feeding a busy, hungry family with different tastes and wanting to include more meat-free meals into the weekly menu, she set out to create a series of budget-friendly, seasonal and make-ahead vegetarian and vegan dishes that will appeal to everyone. *The Green Batch Cook Book* is packed with gloriously mouth-watering meal prep ideas for every cook.

Also by Sam Gates

The Tin & Traybake Cookbook
The Batch Cook Book

Sam Gates

The Green Batch Cook Book

WITH PHOTOGRAPHY BY SAM GATES

ROBINSON

ROBINSON

First published in Great Britain in 2022
by Robinson

10 9 8 7 6 5 4 3 2 1

A CIP catalogue record for this book
is available from the British Library.

ISBN 978-1-47214-708-0

Typeset in Alegreya and Alegreya Sans
designed by Juan Pablo del Peral

Book designed by Andrew Barron at Thextension

Printed and bound in Great Britain
by Bell & Bain Limited

Papers used by Robinson are from well-managed
forests and other responsible sources.

MIX
Paper from
responsible sources
FSC® C104740

Robinson
An imprint of
Little, Brown Book Group
Carmelite House
50 Victoria Embankment
London EC4Y 0DZ

An Hachette UK Company
www.hachette.co.uk
www.littlebrown.co.uk

HOW TO BOOKS are published by Robinson,
an imprint of Little, Brown Book Group.
We welcome proposals from authors who
have first-hand experience of their subjects.
Please set out the aims of your book, its target
market and its suggested contents in an email to
howto@littlebrown.co.uk

Acknowledgements

For Andrew.

With huge thanks to all my wonderful recipe testers:

Tallulah and Jack Storm, Helier Bowling, Lauren Brauer, Karen Brooks, Carol Bysshe, Karen Davies, Vicky and Daisy Evans, Emma Ferrier, Kerry Florin, Mariangela and Diana Franchetti, Emma Harrison, Lizzie Holohan, Katie Horne, Emma Howard, Polly Howard, Lisa Inglis, Caroline Newall, Lauren Newhouse, Jess Palmer, Jenny Parrish, Sasha and John Pattinson, Tanya Prior, Sacha Smith, Desi Stoeva, Ned and Oscar Trier, Paula Valadas, Natalie Wheeler and Daisy Wright.

Thank you to picture editor Kasia Fiszer; my lovely editor, Tom Asker; and the team at Little, Brown: Amanda Keats, Laura Nickoll, Andrew Barron, Abby Marshall and Jess Gulliver.

Contents

Chapter 3
Everyday feasts 88

Chapter 4
Family-friendly big batches 130

Chapter 5
Sweets and treats 168

Chapter 6
Leftovers, gluts and things in jars 202

Index 220

Ⓥ

All the recipes in this book are vegetarian or
vegan. Those which are vegan, or have vegan
ingredient options, are marked as shown.

Introduction

The phenomenal rise in the popularity of veganism, plant-based meals and flexitarian diets means that more of us are regularly choosing to cook meat-free dishes. Concerns about waste and budgets have driven us to make conscious decisions about avoiding waste, and root-to-shoot eating is becoming more mainstream. Whether it's planning menus and shopping lists to avoid unnecessary trips to the supermarket, finding new ways to use leftovers, or eating healthier food, how and what we eat has moved firmly into centre stage.

But, as traditional batch-cook recipes tend to lean towards vats of mince, finding ideas for brilliant make-ahead meat-free dishes isn't always easy. When I wrote *The Batch Cook Book*, I was on a bit of a mission to redefine the concept. For too long I felt batch cooking had been symbolised by soggy shepherd's pies lurking in the freezer. As a working mum, I was more than familiar with being too tired to cook after a long day, but I also knew that things could be different. Batch cooking should be about making gorgeous everyday food when you have the time, that you can eat and enjoy when you don't. So, by changing the perception of what can be made ahead, we can move from uninspired bulk cooking to creating colourful, vibrant, delicious meals that demand to be relished whenever you're ready for them.

What I didn't expect was the success of the vegetable recipes in *The Batch Cook Book*. It began in the early stages, when many of my regular recipe testers specifically requested only vegetarian and vegan recipes. Although we aren't vegetarian or vegan, like many families, we've been choosing to eat meat-free meals more often, so I knew they would be in demand. I probably shouldn't have been surprised at how easy it was to create excellent, freezable big-batch vegetable dishes, or how popular they would become.

Our tastes are constantly evolving and having meat-eaters, vegetarians and vegans around the kitchen table at every meal is now the norm, but finding recipes that will keep everyone happy without exhausting the cook can be a challenge.

That's where *The Green Batch Cook Book* comes in. Delicious vegetarian and vegan batch-cook dishes don't just make the shopping and cooking less stressful by saving you time, they create precious common ground in the kitchen, giving noisy, hungry groups with differing tastes the space to co-exist harmoniously.

From beautiful brunches and lunches that lift your day, evening meals that welcome you home with an edible hug, or family-sized feasts for precious times when you can gather together, these innovative make-ahead recipes harness the vibrant flavours of fruit and vegetables. Most recipes can be halved, or you can make the full batch, eat them over two mealtimes and re-purpose the leftovers. They are all so good that I guarantee no one will feel short-changed.

Modern batch cooking isn't just about making a load of pasta sauce or puréeing vegetables for the freezer. And it's definitely not about complicated shopping lists and strict meal-prep calendars that exhaustively dictate when and what you should eat. It's about making life easier and capturing fresh flavours in glorious, vibrant dishes that you will want to make and eat day after day.

Cooking in advance saves time and money as well as helping to reduce waste, and it's more important than ever before. When you need food fast, but the fridge is full of scrag ends and dubious leftovers, your go-to emergency meal might be beans on toast, veggie burgers and frozen peas, or a stash of dried noodles and a bottle of soy sauce. They're all edible and occasionally tasty, but if you're looking for more than just a quick fix for hunger pangs, make-ahead meals are the answer. And there are plenty of other reasons why it's a good idea to make batch cooking and meal prep a regular part of your weekly routine:

Bespoke batches
Batch cooks aren't just for suppers. Batch-cook breakfasts if you're not a morning person, stockpile lunches if you're always on the go, or build a helpful cake stash for friends who need tea and sympathy.

Batch basics
Spend a little me-time prepping sauces for the freezer. It's easy and quick to transform a classic tomato sauce or a humble white sauce into a delicious meal.

Keep it cosy
Small batches are ideal when you're on your own. Make 4 servings and freeze in single portions.

Cook once, eat twice
The batch-cook's mantra. Double up your favourite recipe, eat one serving and freeze the other.

Baby batches
Fill ice-cube trays with simple foods, such as puréed vegetables or fruit, for a ready supply of healthy, tasty food in tiny-tummy-sized portions.

Beautiful batches
Don't be put off by adventurous recipes. Set aside time for a special baking project and freeze the results for special occasions.

Cooking for crowds
Want to be in the room where it all happens? Batch cook industrial-sized dishes in advance and you can join the party too.

Batch on track

Need to stay away from certain foods? Stock up on delicious meals that fit the way you want to eat and never feel short-changed by limited offerings when you're out and about.

Above all, planning your meal prep and batch cooks doesn't need to be stressful. Inside this book you'll find over 70 straightforward and mouth-watering new recipes that will help you fill your fridge and freezer with delicious meals. All you'll need to do is set aside a little time and enjoy the creative process.

The secret to successful batch cooking is to cook more of what you love when you have the time, so you can eat delicious, fabulous food when you don't.

Cook's notes

1 Use salted butter.

2 Use medium-sized eggs, fruit and vegetables unless otherwise specified.

3 Use whole or semi-skimmed milk, but not skimmed.

4 Use fresh herbs unless the recipe calls for dried.

5 Onions and garlic are peeled unless otherwise specified.

6 Leeks and spring onions are trimmed.

7 Wash all vegetables and fruit before use.

8 All lemons used for zesting should be unwaxed.

9 When cooling cooked rice to store, cool it quickly (within 1 hour), then seal in an airtight container and chill or freeze as soon as possible.

Money-saving tips

With a little planning, meal prep and batch cooking can make a big difference to your food budget.

1. Instead of buying whatever catches your eye on a last-minute supermarket dash, go shopping with recipes in mind and a good idea of the quantities you will need.

2. Buy-one-get-one-free offers sound good, but if you don't have a plan for those extra ingredients, it can cost you more when they end up in the bin. Include them in batch-cook recipes to ensure nothing is wasted.

3. Seasonal shopping. It doesn't just make environmental sense to buy seasonal produce, it's cheaper too.

4. Buy in bulk. Using the same ingredients in different dishes can make a real difference to your pocket. Tinned foods such as tomatoes, beans and pulses are ideal.

5. Preserve nature's bounty. Forage for wild herbs, hedgerow berries and windfall apples and pears when they are plentiful, and preserve their sweet flavours for leaner days by drying, freezing or stewing.

6. Recycle your leftovers. Turn peel and vegetable trimmings into healthy, preservative-free stocks or turn unwanted crusts into breadcrumbs.

7. Store and freeze food and ingredients in portion sizes so you can save on waste and defrost only what you need.

The big freeze

The freezer is the batch cook's best friend, a happy place where you can store those home-cooked meals and the single ingredients to kickstart your day-to-day cooking.

Just as it's not worth hoarding clothes, hoping they'll be back on trend one day, it's not worth hanging onto old food either. Start with a ruthless freezer edit, and when the freezer is sparkling clean and ready to fill up, use these helpful tips to keep things running smoothly.

1. Freezers like being full. It makes them run more efficiently, so as soon as it's ready, fill it up!

2. Store liquids such as stocks, soups, sauces and stews in reusable freezer bags, laid flat and stacked on top of each other. This helps maximise available space and allows fillings to defrost evenly without getting stuck in those pesky corners.

3. Open-freeze bean balls, berries and cookie portions. Lay them flat on a reusable liner on a baking tray and freeze until solid. Transfer to airtight bags or boxes and freeze efficiently.

4. Score traybakes and fruit bars into equal slices before freezing. It'll make it easier to remove them from the freezer if you need only a few portions.

5. Label everything! It's tricky to keep track of everything you've cooked, and many frozen foods look alike, so make sure you write names and dates on the packaging before freezing.

6. Freeze in portions. Cut down on waste by dividing your batch-cooked dishes into portions for one, two or more so you don't have to defrost more than you need. And if you're cooking for different appetites, add child-sized, adult or extra-hungry labels!

Batch-prep storage

To help cut down on waste and single-use plastics, try to avoid those traditional food-storage bags that come with little wire ties. From silicone freezer bags, glass boxes and sustainable, compostable packaging to the humble shower cap, you won't have to look too hard to find planet-friendlier alternatives. Here are a few suggestions:

1 Buy self-sealing, good quality bags and re-use them. When they are empty, wash carefully with warm soapy water and turn inside out to dry.

2 Re-use your other plastic bags and containers. If they don't have air holes, many bread and vegetable bags can be washed and re-used. Every time you do this, it's one less plastic bag in landfill.

3 Invest in reusable freezer bags, which can be used numerous times before recycling. You can also use them for packed lunches, cupboard storage and marinating.

4 Reusable silicone lids can be stretched over bowls and containers instead of cling film.

5 Use airtight containers, such as Tupperware or Lock & Lock. Buy a stacking set to save on storage space.

6 For large bakes, such as lasagne, line the baking dish with cling film or reusable (freezable) wrapping. Place the uncooked bake inside, fold the wrapping over the top and freeze until just solid. Remove the wrapped bake and slide into a reusable bag for freezing. To cook, remove the cling film or reusable wrapping and slide it back into the baking dish.

7 Glass Pyrex-style dishes with airtight plastic lids are reusable and excellent for cutting down on washing up. Simply defrost, remove the lid and bake.

8 Silicone muffin moulds create perfect single portions of soups, sauces and sides. Fill the muffin holes and freeze until the contents are solid enough to stack, then tip the portions into bags or boxes.

9 Stock up on extra ice-cube trays and freeze cooking-sized amounts of sauces, wine, gravies and stock.

10 For easy portioning of cakes and bakes, use square and rectangular traybake tins.

11 Beeswax wraps aren't just reusable, they are compostable too! Use them to wrap sandwiches or to seal dishes for the fridge.

12 Buy a shower cap for the kitchen! Washable plastic shower caps are useful for quick fridge storage. The elastic forms a loose seal around containers, keeping the contents fresh.

1 | Batch breakfasts

Why is it that time seems to speed up in the mornings? Breakfast may be the most important meal of the day, but during the week there's rarely time for more than a quick bowl of cereal or a slice of toast eaten on the run. Getting a nutritious, balanced start to your busy day is not always a priority when you are trying to leave the house with everything you need or are starting work at home.

It's a different story at the weekends. Without the clock-watching, breakfast can afford to be a lazier, more luxurious affair, full of indulgent ingredients and treats. It all seems a bit unfair. Weekdays are when we usually work the hardest and have the most stress, so wouldn't it be great if we could have a little more joy then too?

There is a way to get a better balance. Breakfast is the meal that people least associate with batch cooking, but trust me, it's a game-changer. So many breakfast recipes can be prepared or made ahead, ready to deliver a healthy, filling and adventurous start to the day whether you're racing to the car or planning a leisurely Sunday fry-up.

From fruit bars, Marmite toast or chunky frittata slices to showstopper frozen quiches or rose-pink rhubarb and custard pancakes, batch cooking can't hit the snooze button on your busy mornings, but it can give you the breakfast you deserve, every day of the week.

Breakfasts

Hash brown breakfast quiche with spinach and tomatoes

Rich olive and tomato toast toppers ⓥ

Giant mushrooms with a crunchy herb filling ⓥ

Leek, chive and cheese croquettes

Golden polenta slices with caramelised sherry tomatoes

No-knead Marmite and cheese loaf

Green chilli cheese cornbread

Summer herb and potato farls ⓥ

Sweet potato, pepper and feta frittata

Rose-pink rhubarb and vanilla custard pancakes

Brown sugar and cranberry rusks

Rocket fuel apricot and cranberry bars ⓥ

Hash brown breakfast quiche with spinach and tomatoes

This is an ingenious way of serving up an excellent gluten-free cooked breakfast in a handily edible dish. The sunny, rich quiches look gorgeous and freeze well, so it's definitely worth making a few batches in advance to stash away for busy mornings

FEEDS 8 (MAKES 2 QUICHES)

FOR THE POTATO CASE

600g/1lb 5oz gluten-free frozen hash browns, defrosted
80g/2¾oz strong cheddar, grated
1 tbsp chopped thyme leaves
1 tbsp chopped chives
1 egg, beaten
¼ tsp paprika
salt and black pepper

FOR THE FILLING

1 tbsp sun-dried tomato oil
1 red onion, thinly sliced into rings
6 eggs, beaten
200ml/7fl oz whole milk
100g/3½oz frozen whole-leaf spinach, defrosted, chopped and drained
100g/3½oz cheddar, grated
6 sun-dried tomatoes in oil, drained and thinly sliced

1 Thoroughly grease two 20cm (8in) loose-bottomed sandwich tins and line the bases with greaseproof paper.

2 Tip the hash browns into a mixing bowl and break them up completely. Add the cheese, herbs, egg, paprika and plenty of salt and pepper.

3 Press the mixture over the base and up the sides of the tins, making sure there are no gaps for the filling to leak through. Press the bottom of a glass on the potato mixture at the base of the tin and roll the glass around the sides of the tin to create an even surface.

4 Place the tins in the freezer for 1 hour to allow the cases to firm up.

5 Preheat the oven to 200°C fan (220°C/425°F/ Gas mark 7).

6 Bake the frozen bases in the oven for 15 minutes, then remove and set aside to cool. Reduce the oven temperature to 170°C fan (190°C/375°F/Gas mark 5).

7 Heat the sun-dried tomato oil in a small frying pan over a medium heat, add the onion rings and fry gently for 6–8 minutes. Set aside.

8 Mix the eggs, milk, spinach and cheese in a mixing bowl, season with salt and pepper, then stir in the onion rings.

9 Pour the egg filling into the cooled cases and scatter the sliced sun-dried tomatoes over the top.

10 Bake in the oven for 20–25 minutes, until lightly golden and set.

To freeze allow to cool completely then wrap in foil, cling film or reusable (freezable) wrapping. The dish can be frozen for up to 1 month. Unwrap and cook from frozen for 30 minutes at 200°C fan (220°C/425°F/ Gas mark 7).

Rich olive and tomato toast toppers Ⓥ

Bruschetta is usually made with fresh tomatoes and makes for a gorgeous breakfast, particularly in the summer. But what if you have a craving for those sun-kissed flavours in the winter? This is the answer. Slow roasting tinned tomatoes sounds crazy, but they make a luxuriously rich and chunky topping you can use straight away or mix with chopped olives for extra texture and flavour. Six tins of tomatoes sounds excessive, but they reduce down to a very manageable quantity!

FEEDS 4

6 x 400g/14oz tins plum tomatoes
4 tbsp olive oil, plus extra for brushing
8 thyme sprigs
10 olives, stones removed, and cut into slivers
30g/1oz basil leaves
8 small slices of rustic bread
salt and black pepper

1 Preheat the oven to 150°C fan (170°C/340°F/ Gas mark 3) and line a large roasting tin with greaseproof paper or a reusable non-stick liner.

2 Place a sieve or colander over a large bowl or saucepan and drain the tinned tomatoes. The juice will keep in the fridge for up to 2 days and is excellent for adding to sauces or soups instead of water (such as the Universal Vegan Base on page 144 or Slow-roasted Tomato Soup on page 54).

3 Remove any particularly woody stalks from the tomatoes – this is a messy business, so I find it easiest to use scissors. Roughly scrape out and discard any big clumps of seeds.

4 Place the tomatoes on the lined roasting tin. Splay the tomatoes out on the tray and gently flatten the bigger tomatoes to make them all roughly the same height. Drizzle the olive oil over the top and scatter with the thyme sprigs. Season with salt and pepper.

5 Roast in the oven for 1 hour 30 minutes, until the tomatoes are firm and have lost their sloppiness.

6 Allow to cool, then remove and discard the thyme sprigs. Roughly chop the tomatoes and tip them into a bowl along with any pan juices. Stir in the olives.

7 Reserve a few basil leaves for serving, then tear the remainder into small pieces and stir into the tomatoes. Taste and season with more salt and pepper if desired.

8 To serve, lightly toast the bread and brush with olive oil. Spoon the warm tomato mixture on top and scatter with the remaining basil leaves.

The topping will keep in the fridge for up to 2 days. To freeze, allow to cool completely and freeze in an airtight container for up to 2 months.

Giant mushrooms with a crunchy herb filling ⓥ

Stuffed mushrooms are well known as a classic vegetarian main course, but they make a surprisingly indulgent breakfast too. This recipe can handily be made up to 24 hours before roasting, so you can prepare the mushrooms the night before. If you're feeling a bit delicate the next morning, all you need to do is pop them in the oven and nurse a coffee while you await your feast.

FEEDS 4

8 large open-cup mushrooms
4 tbsp oil from a jar of sun-dried tomatoes in oil, plus extra for drizzling
20g/¾oz flat-leaf parsley, leaves and stalks chopped separately
1 leek, finely chopped
150g/5½oz fine breadcrumbs
12 sun-dried tomatoes in oil, drained and finely chopped
80g/2¾oz mature cheddar or vegan alternative, grated
2 tbsp olive oil, plus extra for greasing
salt and black pepper

1 Preheat the oven to 180°C fan (200°C/400°F/ Gas mark 6) and grease a large baking tray.

2 Cut the mushroom stems from the mushrooms and chop them finely.

3 Heat the 4 tablespoons of sun-dried tomato oil in a small frying pan over a medium-high heat, add the chopped mushroom stems, chopped parsley stalks, chopped leek and a good pinch of salt and cook for 6–8 minutes.

4 Add the breadcrumbs and fry for 5 minutes until lightly golden.

5 Remove the pan from the heat and stir in the chopped sun-dried tomatoes, half of the chopped parsley leaves and half of the grated cheddar or vegan alternative. Season well with salt and pepper.

6 Spoon equal amounts of filling into each mushroom cup, pressing it down lightly. Scatter with the remaining cheddar (or vegan alternative).

7 Drizzle the olive oil over the mushrooms and roast in the oven for 15–20 minutes, until crisp and golden on top.

8 Scatter the remaining chopped parsley leaves over the mushrooms before serving.

To make ahead, prepare the mushrooms as above but do not bake. Cover and keep for up to 2 days in the fridge. Roast as above.

Leek, chive and cheese croquettes

This wonderfully indulgent breakfast or brunch dish takes a little time, so it's ideal for making in big batches in advance and freezing until the right occasion comes along. It's one of my favourite breakfasts, especially when served with poached eggs and grilled tomatoes. I leave the potato skins on, but feel free to remove them if you prefer.

FEEDS 4–6

400g/14oz leeks, thinly sliced
50g/1¾oz butter
350g/12oz potatoes, scrubbed and cut into
    small chunks
1 tbsp Dijon mustard
120g/4oz mature cheddar, finely grated
30g/1oz chives, finely chopped
3 eggs
200g/7oz fine breadcrumbs
plain flour, for dusting
olive oil, for frying
salt and black pepper

1 Place the leeks and butter in a large non-stick frying pan and add a pinch of salt. Cook gently over a medium heat for 10–12 minutes until the leeks have become translucent and any liquid has evaporated. Set aside to cool for 5 minutes.

2 While the leeks are softening, place the potatoes in a pan of water and bring to the boil. Boil for 8–10 minutes until cooked through, then drain and mash in the pan. Stir in the mustard, grated cheese and two-thirds of the chopped chives. Season well with salt and pepper.

3 Beat 2 of the eggs and stir them into the mash, then add the cooled leeks and half the breadcrumbs and mix well.

4 Line a baking tray with greaseproof paper or a reusable liner.

5 Using floured hands, shape and lightly roll the mixture into 12 equal sausage shapes and place them on the lined baking tray. Try to roll the croquettes as gently as possible to avoid making them too dense. Place the tray of croquettes in the fridge for 30 minutes to firm up.

6   When you are ready to cook, heat the oven to
    180°C fan (200°C/400°F/Gas mark 6).

7   Beat the remaining egg in a small bowl. Place
    the remaining breadcrumbs in another bowl.
    Roll a croquette in the beaten egg, then roll it
    in the breadcrumbs and place back on the
    tray. Repeat with all the croquettes.

8   Heat 2 tablespoons of olive oil in a large frying
    pan over a medium heat. Add 6 croquettes and
    fry for 8–10 minutes, turning them
    occasionally until they are lightly golden on
    each side. Remove from the pan, place them
    back on the tray and keep warm, then repeat
    the process with the remaining croquettes,
    adding more oil when needed.

9   Place the tray in the oven and bake for
    12–15 minutes until golden brown and piping
    hot inside.

To freeze the cooked croquettes, allow to cool
completely, then place in an airtight box or
bag and freeze for up to 2 months. Reheat
from frozen at 180°C fan (200°C/400°F/Gas
mark 6) for 30–35 minutes until piping hot.

Golden polenta slices with caramelised sherry tomatoes

Deeply cheesy polenta slices with burnished edges, topped with intensely flavoured tomatoes – what's not to like? These are colours and flavours that will make your heart sing and brighten up any kind of day. This recipe makes a large quantity of polenta, but don't worry, because the extra slices can be frozen for future feasts.

FEEDS 8

FOR THE POLENTA

2 tbsp olive oil, plus extra for cooking
    and greasing
¼ tsp salt
300g/10½oz instant polenta
120g/4oz Red Leicester cheese, grated
80g/2¾oz mature cheddar, grated
2 tbsp chopped thyme leaves
2 tbsp chopped flat-leaf parsley leaves
black pepper

FOR THE CARAMELISED SHERRY TOMATOES

16 plum tomatoes
2 tbsp runny honey
4 tbsp olive oil
3 tbsp sherry vinegar
10 thyme sprigs, leaves picked
salt and black pepper

1 First, make the polenta. Grease a large (about 20 x 30cm/8 x 12in) rectangular dish or baking tray with olive oil.

2 Bring 1.3 litres of water to the boil in a large pan and add the olive oil and salt. When the water is boiling, remove the pan from the heat and stir in the polenta. Mix quickly and firmly with a wooden spoon until the polenta has absorbed all the water.

3 Turn the heat down to medium and return the pan to the hob, stirring the polenta continuously for 3 minutes. Turn the heat off and speedily beat in the grated cheese, herbs and plenty of black pepper. Keep stirring until it is completely absorbed. Pour the polenta into the greased dish and gently smooth the top. Leave to cool and set.

4 Once it has set, cut the polenta into squares or triangles and cook as below or freeze it between layers of greaseproof paper or reusable non-stick liners for up to 1 month.

5 To make the tomatoes, preheat the oven to 130°C fan (150°C/300°F/Gas mark 2).

6 Halve the tomatoes lengthways and place on a large baking tray.

7   In a small bowl, whisk the honey, oil and
    vinegar together. Set aside half of the thyme
    leaves and stir the rest into the honey, oil and
    vinegar mixture. Season well with salt and
    pepper. Pour the mixture over the tomatoes
    and gently mix until they are evenly coated.
    Arrange them so they are cut side down.

8   Roast in the oven for 50 minutes–1 hour until
    soft. Remove from the oven and turn the
    tomatoes so they are lying cut side up.

9   Turn off the oven and preheat the grill to a hot
    setting. Place the tomatoes under the hot grill
    for 4–5 minutes until the cut sides are nicely
    caramelised. Turn off the grill and leave the
    tomatoes in the still-warm oven while you fry
    the polenta.

10 Heat 2 tablespoons of oil in a large non-stick
    frying pan over a medium-high heat. Place as
    many polenta squares or triangles as you can
    fit in the pan without touching and fry for
    4–6 minutes on each side until golden, crisp
    and piping hot. Fry the remaining slices.

11 To serve, spoon the roasted tomatoes and any
    juices on top, scatter with the reserved thyme
    leaves and dish up with a side order of spinach
    or rocket if desired.

No-knead Marmite and cheese loaf

This super-easy loaf requires nothing more than a quick whisk and stir of the ingredients before baking. The loaf turns a gorgeous caramel colour when baked and is delicious eaten fresh and warm from the oven or toasted. There is nothing wrong with a double Marmite experience as far as I'm concerned – I've even been known to spread another layer of Marmite on top of each slice.

MAKES 1 LOAF

2 tsp Marmite
1 tsp Dijon mustard
4 tbsp olive oil
150g/5½oz Greek yoghurt
3 eggs, beaten
1 tbsp finely chopped flat-leaf parsley
120g/4oz extra-mature cheddar, grated
200g/7oz plain flour
2 tsp baking powder
½ tsp bicarbonate of soda
½ tsp poppy seeds
black pepper

1 Preheat the oven to 180°C fan (200°C/400°F/ Gas mark 6) and line the base and sides of a 2lb/900g loaf tin with greaseproof paper or a reusable loaf-tin liner.

2 Whisk the Marmite, mustard, oil, yoghurt and eggs in a large mixing bowl. Add a generous grind of black pepper and the chopped parsley. Stir in 100g/3½oz of the grated cheddar, reserving the rest for the top of the loaf.

3 Mix the flour, baking powder and bicarbonate of soda together. Pour the dry mixture into the wet ingredients and stir just until you can't see any white flour streaks.

4 Tip the bread mixture into the lined tin and scatter the reserved cheese evenly over the top. Sprinkle the poppy seeds over the cheese and bake in the oven for 45–50 minutes, or until a cake tester inserted into the middle of the loaf comes out clean.

If you aren't eating the bread straight away, allow it to cool and wrap it in foil or reusable wrapping. It will keep at room temperature for up to 3 days.

To freeze, cool the loaf completely and wrap it tightly in foil or reusable (freezable) wrapping. Freeze for up to 1 month. The loaf can also be frozen in slices. Separate the slices with baking paper or reusable wrappings, freeze, then just pop straight into the toaster.

Green chilli cheese cornbread

A quick and pleasingly golden little loaf that works for breakfast, brunch or lunch. It's made with mild fresh green chilli so it's not hugely spicy, but if you prefer a gentler start to your day, use just one chilli, not two.

MAKES 1 LOAF

100g/3½oz plain flour
120g/4oz instant polenta
1 tbsp baking powder
1 tsp salt
2 eggs
284ml/9¾fl oz carton of buttermilk or 284g/
    10oz Greek yoghurt
60g/2¼oz melted butter, plus extra for greasing
80g/2¾oz extra-mature cheddar, grated
1–2 green chillies, deseeded and finely chopped
2 tbsp finely chopped chives
black pepper

1 Preheat the oven to 180°C fan (200°C/400°F/ Gas mark 6). Grease a large (900g/2lb) loaf tin with butter and line the base and sides with greaseproof paper or a reusable non-stick loaf-tin liner.

2 Mix the flour, polenta and baking powder in a bowl. Stir in the salt and a generous grind of black pepper.

3 Whisk the eggs, buttermilk (or yoghurt) and melted butter together in a separate bowl, then pour it into the flour mixture and mix well.

4 Set aside a handful of grated cheese for the top, then tip the remaining cheese, chilli and chives into the wet mixture and mix to combine.

5 Pour the bread mixture into the lined tin and bake in the oven for 40 minutes. Sprinkle with the reserved cheese and bake for another 5–10 minutes until the loaf is nicely risen and golden brown. Check with a cake tester, inserting it into the middle of the bread: if it comes out clean it is ready.

6 Remove from the oven and leave to cool and firm up in the tin for 10 minutes, then turn out onto a cooling rack.

If you can resist the temptation to eat it all in one sitting, the loaf can also be frozen whole or in slices. To freeze the whole loaf, allow to cool completely, then wrap tightly in foil or reusable (freezable) wrapping and freeze for up to 2 months. To freeze in slices, separate the slices with baking paper or reusable wrappings, freeze, then just pop straight into the toaster.

Summer herb and potato farls Ⓥ

Potato farls make an excellent bed for your favourite breakfast ingredients and a great alternative to toast. The farls are made with lots of green summer herbs for a zesty, fresh flavour and are especially good topped with mushrooms or grilled tomatoes. This recipe is also very useful for using up any leftover mash.

FEEDS 4 (MAKES 8 FARLS)

500g/1lb 2oz potatoes, ideally Maris Piper, peeled and quartered
50g/1¾oz butter or vegetable spread, plus extra for cooking
80g/2¾oz plain flour, plus extra for dusting
½ tsp baking powder
2 tbsp finely chopped chives
2 tbsp finely chopped flat-leaf parsley leaves
salt and black pepper

1 Cook the potatoes in boiling water for 12–15 minutes until cooked through. Drain, then place back in the hot saucepan.

2 Pass the potatoes through a potato ricer or mash as smoothly as you can by hand. Add the butter or spread and season with plenty of salt and pepper.

3 Mix the flour and baking powder together and stir it into the potato. Scatter the fresh herbs over the mash and mix well.

4 Lightly dust a flat surface with flour and tip the potato mix on top. Form it into a rough ball and cut it into two pieces. Set one aside.

5 Roll the first ball out into a circle about 15cm (6in) wide and 1cm (½in) thick. Lightly dust the circle with flour and cut into quarters, so you end up with 4 triangle-shaped farls. Place the farls on greaseproof paper and repeat the process with the remaining mash.

6 To cook the farls, heat a little butter or spread in a non-stick frying pan over a medium-high heat. Add the farls, making sure they don't touch, and cook for 3–4 minutes on each side until golden brown and piping hot.

To freeze the uncooked farls, lay them on greaseproof paper or reusable non-stick liner on a baking tray and open freeze for 30–40 minutes. Remove the farls from the tray and place them in airtight containers or bags between layers of greaseproof paper or reusable liners. To cook from frozen, follow the same frying instructions above, but allow 6–8 minutes each side.

Sweet potato, pepper and feta frittata

This colourful, generous frittata is a doddle to make and tastes divine hot or cold. It's especially good for eating on the run or on road trips, as it holds together beautifully. Just wrap a few warm slices in foil (or beeswax wrap/other reusable wrapper) to take with you to munch on happily when hunger strikes. If you can find some sour or tangy chutney to enjoy alongside, so much the better.

FEEDS 6–8

300g/10½oz sweet potatoes, peeled and cut
    into bite-sized pieces
300g/10½oz potatoes, peeled and cut
    into bite-sized pieces
1 green pepper, deseeded and cut into chunks
1 yellow pepper, deseeded and cut into chunks
2 tbsp olive oil
generous pinch of dried chilli flakes
150ml/5fl oz single cream
5 eggs
150g/5½oz feta
large handful of basil leaves, torn into
    small pieces
30g/1oz mature cheddar, grated
salt and black pepper

1 Preheat the oven to 180°C fan (200°C/400°F/ Gas mark 6).

2 Place the potatoes and peppers on a large baking tray, drizzle with the olive oil and season with salt and pepper. Scatter over the chilli flakes and toss to coat in the oil. Roast in the oven for 40 minutes, until the potatoes are cooked and golden brown around the edges.

3 Whisk the cream with the eggs in a bowl and season well with salt and pepper. Crumble the feta into the mixture and add half of the torn basil leaves.

4 Tip the vegetables and any oil left in the baking tray into a large non-stick frying pan set over a low heat. Pour the egg mixture over the top and shake the pan gently so that it sits in an even layer. Scatter the grated cheddar evenly over the top.

5 Cook over a low heat without stirring for 8–10 minutes until the frittata begins to set around the sides and the base. While it is setting, preheat the grill.

6 Place the frittata under the hot grill and cook for 3–4 minutes until the top sets and turns golden. Remove from the heat and set aside for 5 minutes to firm up, then scatter with the remaining basil leaves. Serve hot or cold.

If you are making in advance, allow the frittata to cool completely, then wrap in foil, reusable wrapping or cling film and chill for up to 3 days.

Rose-pink rhubarb and vanilla custard pancakes

Who doesn't love pancakes? My family love the traditional lemon and sugar-topped variety but are open to new ideas, so we often try different flavours and fillings. This is my pancake version of the classic pudding combo, rose-pink rhubarb and sunshine yellow custard, and we loved it. The pancakes can also be frozen so you can make a batch in advance to save precious time in the mornings.

FEEDS 4

FOR THE RHUBARB
300g/10½oz pink forced rhubarb, cut into
    4cm (1½in) batons
60g/2¼oz caster sugar

FOR THE PANCAKES
100g/3½oz plain flour
20g/¾oz custard powder
2 large eggs, beaten
½ tsp vanilla extract
200ml/7fl oz milk
40g/1½oz butter, melted, plus extra for cooking
Greek yoghurt, to serve

1. Put the rhubarb and sugar in a wide saucepan and add 2 tablespoons of water. Bring to the boil, then turn the heat right down and simmer for 3 minutes. Remove from the heat, cover and leave to cool in the pan.

2. Taste and add a little more sugar if needed.

3. To make the pancake batter, mix the flour and custard powder together in a large bowl. Make a well in the centre and pour in the beaten eggs and vanilla extract. Whisk the egg so that it begins to pull in the flour mixture, and continue whisking until you have incorporated half of the flour into the eggs.

4. Mix the milk with 5 tablespoons of water. Whisk a few spoonfuls of the milk and water mixture into the flour and egg mixture, then continue adding the milk and water gradually, whisking continuously as you draw in the rest of the flour. Keep whisking until you have a smooth batter.

5. Just before you start cooking, stir the melted butter into the batter.

6. To cook the pancakes, heat a teaspoon of butter in a medium non-stick frying pan over a medium-high heat. Swirl it around, and when it is sizzling, add a ladleful of pancake batter. Swirl the batter around the pan until it covers the base, then leave it to cook for 1–2 minutes until golden on the bottom. Flip the pancake and cook the other side for 1 minute. Slide onto a plate and keep warm. Repeat with the remaining batter – the mixture will make about 8 pancakes.

7. Serve the pancakes with a generous quantity of poached rhubarb and a dollop of Greek yoghurt.

The cooled poached rhubarb will keep for up to 2 days in the fridge.

To freeze the pancakes, cool them completely and place them in flat layers between sheets of greaseproof paper or reusable liners. Slide into an airtight bag and freeze. Defrost and reheat gently in a microwave or warm oven for a few seconds before serving.

Brown sugar and cranberry rusks

In South Africa, rusks are a much-loved breakfast snack or afternoon treat. They are hard, crunchy bakes, designed to be dipped and softened in a hot drink before eating. The rusks are baked twice, with an initial bake at a high temperature, then a second long, slow bake, often done overnight. The rusks will keep for up to 5 days in an airtight container and make great presents. Leftovers can be broken into crumbs and used to top crumbles, pies and cakes. This is a generous recipe that makes plenty of rusks.

MAKES 36 RUSKS

750g/1lb 10oz self-raising flour, plus extra
   for dusting
1 tsp baking powder
220g/7¾oz soft dark brown sugar
200g/7oz butter, melted
1 egg, beaten
2 tsp vanilla extract
500ml/17fl oz buttermilk
170g/5¾oz muesli
50g/1¾oz dried cranberries

1   Preheat the oven to 150°C fan (170°C/340°F/Gas mark 3). Line a large (about 20 x 35cm/8 x 14in) roasting tin with greaseproof paper or a reusable liner.

2   Mix the flour and baking powder together in a bowl.

3   Beat the sugar, melted butter, egg and vanilla extract together in a bowl with a wooden spoon (or with an electric mixer), then stir in the buttermilk.

4   Combine the flour mixture with the wet ingredients to create a soft and sticky dough. Do not overmix.

5   Add the muesli and cranberries to the dough and mix until combined.

6   Tip the dough into the lined tin and use floured hands to gently flatten it evenly. Bake in the oven for 1 hour, then remove the tin from the oven and allow the dough to cool for 15 minutes.

7   Reduce the oven temperature to 50°C fan (70°C/160°F/lowest gas mark).

8   While the rusk dough is still in the tin, cut it into 36 slices. Remove the slices and place them on their sides, directly onto the wire rack in the oven. Put the baking tin under the rack to catch any crumbs.

9   Bake the rusks on this very low heat either overnight, or for 6–7 hours, until hard and crunchy.

10 Allow to cool and store in airtight containers for up to 5 days. Dip into your favourite hot drink and enjoy!

Rocket fuel apricot and cranberry bars Ⓥ

These breakfast bars take just a few minutes to make and last for a week in a tin. The combination of dried cranberries and apricots is an ideal balance of sweet and sour, but this is also a versatile and forgiving recipe that works with any dried fruit. I use scissors to cut the apricots into tiny pieces, as it's a lot faster than using a knife.

MAKES 16 BARS

250g/9oz runny honey or maple syrup
50g/1¾oz smooth peanut butter
2 tsp ground flaxseed
80g/2¾oz dried cranberries
80g/2¾oz dried apricots, finely diced
40g/1½oz mixed seeds
250g/9oz porridge oats
40g/1½oz unsalted pistachios, chopped

1 Preheat the oven to 160°C fan (180°C/350°F/ Gas mark 4), and line the base and sides of a 20cm (8in) square loose-bottomed baking tin with greaseproof paper or a reusable liner.

2 Whisk the honey and peanut butter together in a large bowl. Stir in the flaxseed, cranberries, apricots, seeds, oats and half of the chopped pistachios.

3 Dollop the mixture into the lined tin and smooth the top. Sprinkle the remaining pistachios over the top and gently press them into the mixture so that they are roughly level with the rest of the mixture.

4 Bake in the oven for 20 minutes, then remove from the oven and leave to cool in the tin for 20 minutes before cutting into bars.

The bars will keep for up to 1 week in an airtight container. They can also be frozen between sheets of greaseproof paper for up to 2 months.

2 | Batch lunches

Whether you eat at your desk, while you're on the phone or at the kitchen table, lunch is a meal that really matters. It may be nothing more than a 10-minute dash out of the office, an excuse to leave your laptop and take a turn around the kitchen, or a more joyful, leisurely affair with good friends and family, but it's still an important break in our busy days. However long you have and wherever you're taking yours, lunch offers a welcome respite from the action and a chance to reset before time gathers pace and marches you firmly into the afternoon.

When I started work, lunches were always the same: sandwiches or a limp salad grabbed from a supermarket chiller or the closest eatery to the office. I simply didn't have the time or inclination to think ahead, or so I thought. Then I joined a company based on a remote industrial estate with no access to decent food, and out of necessity, fresh, budget-friendly batch lunches very quickly became my best friend.

Unless it's a long, lazy lunch, having a meal that isn't too heavy or makes you feel sluggish all afternoon is so important for your mental and physical wellbeing. Our family are not vegetarian or vegan, but increasingly, our lunches have become so. It wasn't planned, it just happened that way, and with everyone heading off in different directions, making lighter, fresher lunches to go, that could be prepped in advance, made a lot of sense.

Whatever your lunch routine, this chapter is packed with flavour-filled batch-cook recipes to make your lunchtime sing. From the world's easiest baked eggs and unassuming soups with deep flavours, to sunny summer salads and a glorious galette to grab and go, it's time to indulge yourself. Because the recipes can all be made in advance and frozen or chilled until you need them, working hard doesn't have to stop everyday lunches from being a treat.

Batch lunches

Tarragon and Swiss cheese baked eggs

Broad bean and dill toasts ⓥ

Slow-roasted tomato, basil and garlic soup ⓥ

Pea and soft mint soup ⓥ

Green pesto babka

Edamame and spring green potstickers ⓥ

Red onion, walnut and mozzarella slipper bread ⓥ

Sunny root veg spirals ⓥ

Roast lemon carrots with carrot-top and hazelnut pesto ⓥ

Fiery sweetcorn and red pepper cakes with crispy chilli oil ⓥ

Garlicky mushroom and chestnut sausage rolls ⓥ

Beetroot, tarragon and Boursin galette

Roast garlic and lentil salad with caper dressing ⓥ

Maple-glazed beetroot with walnuts and marjoram ⓥ

Green ribbon and bulgur wheat salad with lemon dressing ⓥ

Broccoli, lemon and almond salad ⓥ

Tarragon and Swiss cheese baked eggs

This cute little multi-tasker of a recipe is courtesy of my friend Ned, who is an amazing cook. It works for any time of day, whether as a simple breakfast dish, a great starter or, as it is here, the perfect lunch. Baked eggs might not immediately spring to mind as a batch-cook dish, but they can be prepared a few hours in advance, and after failing to tempt reluctant teenagers to breakfast one morning, I discovered that any leftovers make an excellent tarragon-flavoured egg mayonnaise. Just one tip: don't even think of eating it hot without some crusty bread to mop up the divine yolky sauce.

FEEDS 4

butter, for greasing
4 tsp double cream
3 tarragon sprigs, leaves picked and
    finely chopped
4 eggs
20g/¾oz Gruyère cheese, grated
salt and black pepper

1 Preheat the oven 180°C fan (200°C/400°F/ Gas mark 6). Grease four ramekins with butter and set them on a small baking tray.

2 Put 1 teaspoon of cream into each ramekin and add a scattering of half the chopped tarragon.

3 Break an egg into each ramekin and season with salt and pepper.

4 Top with the grated Gruyère and place in the oven for 10–12 minutes, until the egg is cooked through but still has a slight wobble.

5 Serve sprinkled with the remaining tarragon and more cheese, if desired.

Any uneaten baked eggs can be turned into egg mayonnaise. Allow to cool completely, then scrape the eggs and cheese into a small bowl. Add 1–2 tablespoons of mayonnaise per egg and mash well. Taste and add more salt and pepper if needed.

Broad bean and dill toasts (V)

This is a quick and creamy, soft green topping for lightly toasted bread or crackers and it also makes an excellent dip for raw vegetables. The recipe works equally well with or without cream cheese, so leave it out if you prefer. I usually have frozen broad beans in the freezer, and add frozen peas for extra colour and sweetness, but if you are lucky enough to have access to fresh broad beans and peas, even better!

FEEDS 4

100g/3½oz frozen peas
300g/10½oz frozen broad beans
4 tbsp olive oil, plus extra for drizzling
juice of ½ lemon
2 tbsp finely chopped dill
4 tbsp cream cheese or vegan alternative
   (optional)
salt and black pepper
8 small slices of bread or large baguette slices,
   to serve

1 Put the frozen peas in a heatproof bowl, pour boiling water over the peas and leave for 1 minute before draining.

2 Bring a saucepan of water to the boil and add the frozen broad beans. Cook for 1 minute, then drain and refresh in cold water. Slip off and discard the grey outer skin from the beans.

3 Put the drained peas, beans, olive oil and lemon juice into a small food processor and add a seasoning of salt and pepper. Blitz for just a couple of seconds, until the mixture has a rough paste-like texture, then stir in three-quarters of the chopped dill and the cream cheese or vegan alternative (if using). Taste and add more seasoning if needed.

4 Toast the bread and smother with the bean mixture, then scatter with the reserved dill and drizzle with olive oil.

The topping will keep covered in the fridge for up to 2 days.

Slow-roasted tomato, basil and garlic soup ⓥ

A warm and welcoming all-rounder of a soup. You can make it in the summer with gluts of crimson tomatoes, or out of season when it brings a much-needed richness to even the grimmest of long-life tomatoes. Don't be put off by the quantity of garlic in the ingredients; it's slow roasted too, so it just brings a gentle sweetness to the soup.

FEEDS 6

1kg/2lb 4oz tomatoes, halved horizontally
8 garlic cloves, unpeeled
4 tbsp olive oil
15g/½oz basil, leaves picked, stalks
    finely chopped
2 red onions, finely chopped
2 celery sticks, finely chopped
1 large carrot, grated
3 x 400g/14oz tins chopped tomatoes
1 tbsp maple syrup or honey
salt and black pepper
handful of grated mature cheddar or vegan
    alternative, single cream or chopped chives,
    to serve (optional)

1   Preheat the oven to 150°C fan (170°C/340°F/
    Gas mark 3).

2   Place the tomatoes cut side up on a large
    baking tray and tuck the garlic cloves snugly
    around them. Drizzle with half the olive oil
    and season generously with salt and pepper.
    Jostle the vegetables gently to coat them with
    the seasoned oil.

3   Roast in the oven for 1 hour 10 minutes–1 hour
    30 minutes, until softened and caramelised
    around the edges, basting them with the oil
    and juices halfway through. Remove from the
    oven and set aside until the tomatoes are cool
    enough to handle.

4   While the tomatoes are roasting, heat the
    remaining oil in a large heavy-based saucepan
    or casserole over a medium heat. Add the
    chopped basil stalks, onions, celery, carrot
    and a large pinch of salt and sauté gently for
    10 minutes.

5   Remove the skins and any big stalks from the
    cooled tomatoes and add them to the onion
    mixture. Squeeze the garlic cloves out of their
    skins and into the mixture and add any
    roasting juices.

6   Add the tinned chopped tomatoes, maple
    syrup or honey and a tin of water, and bring
    to the boil, then reduce the heat to a hearty
    simmer and cook for 30–40 minutes until rich
    and syrupy.

7   Remove from the heat, add half of the basil
    leaves and blitz for a few seconds with a stick
    blender to break down any large tomatoes, but
    keeping the rustic, chunky texture. Taste and
    add more seasoning if needed.

8   Top with the remaining herbs and cheese, as
    desired, and add a swirl of cream before
    serving if you're feeling indulgent.

The soup will keep in the fridge for up to
3 days. To freeze, cool completely and store
in an airtight container for up to 2 months.
Defrost and reheat slowly until piping hot.

Pea and soft mint soup ⓥ

This creamy, gentle soup has a delicate summery flavour which is a little misleading, as in our house it's usually made with frozen peas and stock cubes. If you have fresh mint, do use it, but I've made it with dried mint too and no one complained. Serve with a scattering of fresh pea shoots for extra authenticity.

FEEDS 4

40g/1½oz butter or 3 tbsp oil
1 onion, finely chopped
1 litre/34fl oz hot vegetable stock
750g/1lb 10oz frozen peas
20g/¾oz mint leaves, finely chopped,
    or 1 tsp dried mint
100ml/3½fl oz single cream or vegan alternative
salt and black pepper
handful of fresh pea shoots, to serve

1　Melt the butter in a heavy-based saucepan over a medium heat. Add the onion and a pinch of salt and sauté gently for 6–8 minutes until softened.

2　Add the stock and frozen peas and bring to the boil. Reduce the heat and simmer for 5 minutes, then add the chopped mint (or dried mint) and a generous grind of pepper.

3　Remove the pan from the heat, then blitz the soup with a stick blender until it is as smooth as possible. Pour in the cream (or vegan alternative) and gently warm through without boiling. Taste and add more seasoning if needed.

4　Pour into bowls and scatter with fresh pea shoots.

To freeze, cool the soup completely and store in airtight containers for up to 2 months. Defrost, then reheat slowly (without boiling) until piping hot.

Green pesto babka

Babkas are gorgeous, fluffy, swirly loaves that look complicated but are surprisingly easy to make. They are perfect for lunch, eaten soft and meltingly delicious while still warm from the oven or sliced and toasted straight from the freezer.

MAKES 2 LOAVES

500g/1lb 2oz strong white bread flour, plus extra for dusting
7g/¼oz dried quick/instant yeast
1 tsp fine salt
1 tsp caster sugar
160ml/5½fl oz tepid water
160ml/5½fl oz tepid milk
2 tbsp olive oil, plus extra for greasing
1 egg, plus 1 egg yolk for glazing
1 small tub (about 120g/4oz) basil pesto

1 Grease two 450g/1lb loaf tins with oil and line the base and sides with greaseproof paper or a reusable non-stick loaf-tin liner.

2 Mix the flour, yeast, salt and sugar in a large mixing bowl.

3 Whisk the water, milk, oil and egg in a jug then pour it into the dry ingredients. Stir the ingredients together with a flat-bladed knife until it forms a shaggy dough.

4 Lightly flour a work surface. Turn the dough out onto the surface and knead it for 8–10 minutes until smooth and springy, adding a little more flour if needed.

5 Clean and grease the mixing bowl with oil, then return the dough to the bowl and cover with a greased silicone lid or cling film. Leave to rise somewhere warm for 1 hour until doubled in size.

6 Tip the dough out onto the floured surface and cut it in half. Roll both pieces of dough out into separate rectangles, each measuring 40 x 30cm (16 x 12in). Spread the pesto evenly over the two rectangles. Starting from the longest side, roll the first rectangle of dough into a long tube. Repeat with the second rectangle. Cut each tube in half lengthways so that you have four long strips of dough.

7 Turn the halves cut side up so they are lying next to each other. You should be able to just see green lines of pesto running down each one.

8 To plait the loaves, lift the top of one strip of dough and gently place it over the one next to it. Take the strip which is now underneath and place it over the one on the top. Continue to alternate placing dough strips over each other until you have 'plaited' two strips together. Repeat with the two remaining strips of dough. You should now have two long dough plaits. Gently concertina the plaits so that they are short enough to fit into the tins.

9 Carefully lift and place the plaits into the lined tins and cover with greased cling film or reusable wrapping. Leave to rise in a warm place for 40 minutes.

10 Preheat the oven to 180°C fan (200°C/400°F/ Gas mark 6).

11 Remove the cling film or reusable wrapping and brush both loaves with a little beaten egg yolk.

12 Bake in the oven for 30–35 minutes, until the loaves are well risen and lightly golden. Turn out onto a cooling rack and leave for 5 minutes. Eat warm or toasted.

If you can resist the temptation to eat it all in one sitting, the bread can also be frozen whole or in slices. To freeze the whole loaves, allow them to cool completely then tightly wrap in foil, cling film or reusable (freezable) wrapping. Freeze for up to 2 months. Allow to defrost before warming in the oven or toasting. To freeze as slices, separate the slices with baking paper or reusable wrappings, then just pop into the toaster straight from the freezer.

Edamame and spring green potstickers Ⓥ

Emerald green edamame beans make a satisfying dense and crunchy potsticker filling. This recipe was originally created as a way to use up leftover spring greens, and, as it made so many, I decided to freeze some. It worked so well that now I always double the amount and freeze half. Broad beans also work if you can't find edamame.

FEEDS 4

2 tbsp vegetable oil, plus extra for frying
3 spring onions, sliced lengthways and
    finely chopped
2 garlic cloves, crushed
1 green chilli, deseeded and finely chopped
150g/5½oz spring greens, finely shredded
180g/6oz frozen edamame beans
2 tbsp light soy sauce, plus extra for dipping
2 tsp sesame oil
1 tbsp grated fresh ginger
plain flour, for dusting
24 gyoza wrappers

TO SERVE
1 fresh red chilli, thinly sliced
handful of wild garlic or fresh coriander
    leaves, chopped
2 tbsp crispy chilli oil

1 Warm the 2 tablespoons of vegetable oil in a small frying pan over a medium heat, add the spring onions, garlic, chilli and spring greens and cook for 3–4 minutes until softened. Remove from the heat.

2 Cook the edamame beans in boiling water for 3 minutes, then drain and tip them into a small food processor (or a mixing bowl if you don't have a processor). Add the soy sauce, the sesame oil and grated ginger and mix well.

3 Add the onion mixture to the processor and blitz for a few seconds (or mix in the bowl and mash vigorously with a potato masher).

4 Lightly dust a baking tray with flour.

5 To make the potstickers, place a tablespoon of the filling into the centre of a gyoza wrapper. Brush the edge of the wrapper with water all the way around, then crimp the edges together to seal them. Flatten the base slightly and place on the floured baking tray. Repeat until you have made all the 24 potstickers.

6 To freeze the uncooked potstickers, place them onto a baking tray lined with greaseproof paper or a reusable liner. Place in the freezer for 40 minutes to firm up, then tip into airtight freezer bags and freeze for up to 2 months.

➤➤➤

7 To cook, heat 2 tablespoons of vegetable oil in
   a large frying pan (that has a tight-fitting lid)
   over a medium-high heat. Place 12 potstickers
   into the pan, making sure none of them are
   touching each other, and fry for 3–4 minutes
   until the bottoms are crispy and golden.

8 Add 100ml/3½fl oz boiling water to the pan,
   taking care as it will spit and sizzle, and
   quickly cover with a tight-fitting lid. Steam
   for 5–6 minutes, or until the water has been
   absorbed. Set aside and keep warm. Repeat
   the cooking process until all the potstickers
   are cooked.

9 To serve, scatter with sliced chilli, wild garlic
   or coriander leaves, crispy chilli oil and extra
   soy sauce for dipping, if desired.

   The potstickers can be cooked from frozen
   using the same technique as above, but add
   4–6 minutes to the steaming time.

Red onion, walnut and mozzarella slipper bread Ⓥ

This recipe makes a big batch of soft, bouncy, oozy breads that are great as starters or sides. It's inspired by a type of Italian bread called 'pantofola', meaning 'slipper'.

FEEDS 8 (MAKES 4 SLIPPER BREADS)

300ml/10fl oz tepid water

7g/¼oz dried quick/instant yeast

2 tbsp olive oil, plus extra for brushing
    and drizzling

450g/1lb strong white bread flour, plus extra
    for dusting

1 tsp fine salt

½ tbsp caster sugar

2 red onions, thinly sliced into rings

200g/7oz mozzarella or vegan alternative,
    torn into bite-sized pieces

60g/2¼oz chopped walnuts

salt

small handful of parsley leaves, finely chopped,
    to serve

1 Mix the tepid water with the yeast and 1 tablespoon of the olive oil in a bowl.

2 Place the flour, salt and sugar in a large mixing bowl. Make a well in the centre and pour in the yeast mixture. Using a flat-bladed knife, mix the flour with the liquid until it forms a shaggy dough.

3 When the dough starts to come together, turn it out onto a floured surface. Flour your hands and knead the dough for 8–10 minutes until it becomes smooth and silky, adding a little more flour if it becomes too sticky.

4 Clean the mixing bowl and brush it with a little oil. Place the dough back in the bowl and cover with a greased silicone lid or cling film. Place somewhere warm and allow to rise for 50 minutes–1 hour until doubled in size.

5 While the dough is rising, heat the remaining olive oil in a medium frying pan over a low heat, add the sliced onions with a pinch of salt and cook, stirring occasionally, for 20–30 minutes until softened and slightly golden around the edges. Remove from the heat and set aside to cool.

6 Split the dough into four balls and lightly dust two large baking sheets with flour. Roll out a ball of dough on a floured surface into a 30 x 10cm (12 x 4in) oblong. Lift it onto one of the floured baking sheets. Repeat with the remaining balls of dough.

➤➤➤

7   Leaving a 2cm (¾in) border, scatter the middle of each dough 'slipper' with a quarter of the onions, cheese or vegan alternative and chopped walnuts. Fold the borders over slightly to contain the fillings. Cover with greased cling film and leave to rise again, somewhere warm, for 30 minutes.

8   Preheat the oven to 180°C fan (200°C/400°F/ Gas mark 6).

9   Remove the cling film and bake the breads in the oven for 15–20 minutes until puffed up, golden and cooked through. Peek at the underside to check it is cooked before removing from the oven.

10 Drizzle with olive oil, scatter with fresh parsley and serve immediately.

To freeze, allow to cool completely and seal in an airtight bag or box for up to 2 months. Defrost and reheat in the oven for a few minutes before serving.

Sunny root veg spirals ⓥ

These labyrinthine pies are filled with a golden blaze of sunny root vegetables and cool green herbs. They were inspired by the budget-friendly vegetable stew packs you find in supermarkets in colder months. You can swap the swede for butternut squash or pumpkin if that's what you have to hand. The filling can be made up to 24 hours in advance.

MAKES 6

2 tbsp olive oil
1 garlic clove, crushed
1 onion, finely chopped
50g/1¾oz coriander, stalks finely chopped, leaves chopped
1 red chilli, deseeded and finely chopped
20g/¾oz fresh ginger, peeled and finely grated
¼ tsp turmeric
½ tsp ground cumin
½ tsp ground coriander
300g/10½oz swede, cut into 5mm (¼in) dice
1 large carrot, cut into 5mm (¼in) dice
1 medium parsnip, cut into 5mm (¼in) dice
200ml/7fl oz vegetable stock
100g/3½oz frozen peas, defrosted
¼ tsp salt
6 large sheets filo pastry
50g/1¾oz melted butter, or 2 tablespoons olive oil, for greasing
1 tsp mixed seeds
black pepper

1 Heat the oil in a large, deep frying pan over a medium heat, add the garlic, onion and coriander stalks and sauté for 6 minutes, then add the chilli, ginger and dried spices and cook for 2 minutes. Add the diced vegetables and cook over a medium-high heat for a further 10 minutes.

2 Pour in the stock and bring to the boil, then reduce the heat and simmer for 15–20 minutes until the stock is absorbed and the vegetables are tender.

3 Preheat the oven to 180°C fan (200°C/400°F/ Gas mark 6).

4 Remove from the heat and stir in the peas, ¼ teaspoon of salt and plenty of pepper. Stir the chopped coriander leaves through the mixture.

5 To make the spirals, lay the filo sheets in a pile on a work surface. Dip a pastry brush or your fingers in the melted butter or oil and lightly paint the top filo sheet with a thin layer of melted butter or oil. Turn the sheet over and repeat on the other side.

6 Spoon a sixth of the filling mixture across the bottom of the top sheet of filo in an even, sausage-shaped line. Starting from the edge closest to you, roll the sheet with the filling inside into a long tube.

➤➤➤

7 Carefully curl the tube into a spiral and place it on a greased baking tray. Repeat the process until the mixture and filo sheets are finished.

8 Brush the spirals with melted butter or oil, sprinkle with the seeds and bake in the oven for 30–35 minutes until golden and cooked through.

To freeze, cool completely and store in an airtight container for up to 2 months. To reheat the cooked spirals, defrost and place in a preheated oven at 180°C fan (200°C/400°F/Gas mark 6) for 15–20 minutes until crisp and piping hot.

Roast lemon carrots with carrot-top and hazelnut pesto ⓥ

This is a gorgeously colourful recipe which is perfect for lunch or as a sunny side dish. It's very efficient in terms of ingredients as it uses the feathery green carrot tops as well as the carrots themselves. If you can find rainbow carrots to use instead, grab them!

FEEDS 4

2 bunches of fresh carrots with leafy tops, washed
2 tbsp olive oil
grated zest and juice of 1 lemon
1 tbsp runny honey or maple syrup
salt and black pepper

FOR THE CARROT-TOP AND HAZELNUT PESTO
20g/¾oz basil leaves
1 garlic clove
40g/1½oz mature cheddar or vegan alternative, finely grated
150ml/5fl oz olive oil
30g/1oz toasted hazelnuts, finely chopped

1   Preheat the oven to 180°C fan (200°C/400°F/ Gas mark 6).

2   Cut the feathery green tops off the carrots and set them aside for the pesto. Wash the carrots and peel if necessary. If the carrots are very large, cut them lengthways into halves or quarters.

3   Put the carrots into a large baking tin and drizzle with the olive oil. Season with salt and pepper and toss to coat them with the seasoned oil. Roast in the oven for 35 minutes until tender, turning them halfway through.

4   Whisk the lemon juice and honey (or maple syrup) together in a bowl. When the carrots are ready, remove the tin from the oven, toss them in the honey and lemon mixture and return to the oven for 10 minutes.

5   Meanwhile make the pesto. Pick 40g/1½ oz of the youngest, greenest feathery carrot tops from the stalks and discard the rest.

6   Place the tops into a mini food processor. Add the basil, garlic, cheddar (or vegan alternative) and the olive oil. Blitz until it forms a smooth paste. It needs to be loose enough to drop off a spoon, so add a little more oil if needed. Season to taste with salt and pepper.

7   Stir 2 tablespoons of the chopped hazelnuts into the pesto, transfer it to a bowl or jar and cover the top with a thin layer of oil to prevent it from going brown. Set aside.

8   To serve, drizzle 3–4 tablespoons of the pesto over the carrots and sprinkle with the lemon zest and the reserved hazelnuts.

The carrot top pesto can be kept in the fridge for up to 3 days. Leftover carrots are delicious tossed through warm salads or grated into a breakfast hash.

Fiery sweetcorn and red pepper cakes with crispy chilli oil ⓥ

This easy recipe bursts with flavour and has a feisty chilli kick that is brilliant for a quick lunch or breakfast. If you have any young chefs around, get them involved as they can put it together with very little help. This is perfect if you're short on time as the mixture can be made up to 24 hours ahead and kept in the fridge until you're ready to cook.

FEEDS 4

1 x 340g/12oz tin sweetcorn
1 red pepper, deseeded and finely chopped
6 tbsp chives, finely chopped
1 tbsp crispy chilli oil, plus extra for serving
2 eggs, beaten, or 1 flax egg*
3 tbsp plain flour
1 tsp baking powder
vegetable oil, for frying
salt and black pepper

* Mix 1 tablespoon of ground flax seed and 3 tablespoons of boiling water. Leave to stand for 5 minutes.

1 Tip the sweetcorn into a bowl and mash it so that the kernels are broken but still roughly retain their shape. Stir in the red pepper, 4 tablespoons of the chives and the chilli oil. Add the beaten egg (or flax egg) and mix well. Combine the flour and baking powder and add it to the batter. Season generously with salt and pepper and mix well. The mixture can be kept covered in the fridge for up to 24 hours.

2 To cook, heat 1 tablespoon of oil in a non-stick frying pan over a medium-high heat. Add 4 separate heaped tablespoons of the sweetcorn mixture into the pan, making sure they don't touch. Cook for 2–3 minutes, then flip and cook on the other side until lightly golden.

3 Remove and keep warm. Repeat until the mixture is finished. Sprinkle with the remaining chives and drizzle with extra crispy chilli oil.

Garlicky mushroom and chestnut sausage rolls ⓥ

Vegetarian and vegan sausage rolls are all too often stuffed with mean, lacklustre fillings and wrapped in thick, cloying pastry. This is a different story altogether. The rolls are generously packed with layers of sliced mushrooms cooked in wine and herbs, then mixed with mustard and chestnuts. The inspiration came from leftover Christmas chestnuts that I couldn't bear to throw away, but now we buy them just to make the rolls! Slice the mushrooms as thinly as possible, as lots of layers make for a beautifully textured filling.

MAKES 16 ROLLS

4 tbsp olive oil
1 onion, halved and thinly sliced
2 celery sticks, finely diced
3 garlic cloves, crushed
500g/1lb 2oz mixed mushrooms, halved
   (or quartered if large) and thinly sliced
4 tbsp white wine
1½ tbsp wholegrain mustard
80g/2¾oz cooked chestnuts, finely chopped
8 thyme sprigs, leaves picked
1 sheet of ready-rolled all-butter or vegan
   puff pastry
1 beaten egg or a little almond milk, for brushing
1 tbsp white sesame seeds
salt and black pepper

1   Heat 1 tablespoon of the oil in a large, deep frying pan over a medium heat, add the onion and celery with a pinch of salt and cook for 8–10 minutes until softened. Add the crushed garlic and cook for 2 minutes.

2   Turn up the heat to medium-high and add the remaining 3 tablespoons of oil, the mushrooms, and a large pinch of salt. Cook the mushrooms for 10–15 minutes until any juices have evaporated and they are starting to crisp up around the edges.

3   Turn up the heat to high and add the white wine and mustard. Keep stirring until the liquid has been absorbed. Taste and add more salt and pepper if needed. Remove the pan from the heat and tip the contents into a medium mixing bowl.

4   Add the chopped chestnuts and thyme leaves and stir well, then allow to cool.

5   Line a large baking sheet with greaseproof paper or a reusable greaseproof liner.

6   Unroll the puff pastry sheet and cut it in half lengthways so that you have two long strips. Place each strip onto the baking sheet.

7   Working quickly, place equal amounts of the mushroom mixture down the length of each strip of pastry, so that it looks as if you have two long mushroom 'sausages'. Use your hands to gently compress the filling as much as possible so the pastry will fit over the top.

8   Lift one side of the first pastry strip and fold it over the other so that the filling is neatly wrapped inside. Repeat with the other strip.

➤➤➤

9 Press a fork along the edge of each strip where the two sides meet, to seal. Cut each long roll into 8 equal pieces and place them at least 2cm (¾in) apart on the lined baking sheet.

10 If you are baking the rolls now, preheat the oven to 180°C fan (200°C/400°F/Gas mark 6).

11 Paint the rolls with beaten egg (or almond milk) and sprinkle with the sesame seeds. Bake in the oven for 25–30 minutes until nicely puffed up and golden.

To freeze the rolls before baking, do not wash the pastry with egg or milk. Place the baking tray in the freezer for 1 hour to open freeze the uncooked rolls, then place the rolls between layers of greaseproof paper or reusable liners in an airtight container or freezer bag. Freeze for up to 2 months. To cook from frozen, glaze the rolls with beaten egg (or almond milk), sprinkle with sesame seeds and bake as above, adding 10 minutes to the cooking time.

Beetroot, tarragon and Boursin galette

A galette is a wonderfully messy, free-form pie, which looks better the scruffier it is. In this version, rich, flaky pastry loosely cradles a tarragon-scented, deep purple beetroot and leek filling. The top of the galette is dotted with blobs of salty Boursin cheese. This is divine hot, but it also makes a great packed lunch or picnic dish.

FEEDS 4

FOR THE PASTRY

180g/6oz plain flour, plus extra for dusting
¼ tsp fine salt
120g/4oz butter, frozen and grated
5 tbsp cold water

FOR THE FILLING

3 beetroot, scrubbed and trimmed
3 tbsp finely chopped tarragon leaves
30g/1oz butter
2 leeks, sliced into thin medallions
2 tbsp balsamic vinegar
1 tbsp roughly chopped toasted hazelnuts
1–2 tbsp whole milk
100g/3½oz Boursin
salt and black pepper

1 Mix the flour and salt in a mixing bowl. Add the grated butter and mix with a flat-bladed knife. Add the water and continue mixing until it forms a shaggy dough. Bring the dough together and knead it gently on a lightly floured surface, then shape into a flat disc. Wrap in cling film or reusable wrapping and chill for 30 minutes or up to 24 hours. The dough can be frozen at this point.

2 Cook the beetroot in the oven or in a microwave. First, pierce each beetroot several times. To oven-cook, season with salt and pepper, then wrap in foil and roast at 160°C fan (180°C/350°F/Gas mark 4) until tender. To microwave the beetroot, place in a microwavable bowl, cover and microwave for 7–8 minutes until tender.

3 Coarsely grate the cooked beetroot into a mixing bowl. Add 1 tablespoon of the chopped tarragon and mix well.

4 Melt the butter in a small frying pan over a medium heat, add the leeks, another tablespoon of the chopped tarragon and a pinch of salt and fry gently for 8–10 minutes until the leeks are soft. Pour the balsamic vinegar into the pan and cook for 2–3 minutes, then tip the leeks and any melted butter from the pan into the beetroot mixture and mix.

➤➤➤

5 Line a baking sheet with greaseproof paper. Roll the pastry out on a lightly floured surface into a square or circle about 30cm (12in) in diameter.

6 Spread the beetroot and leek mixture across the pastry, leaving a 4cm (1½in) border all around the edge. Fold this border over the edges of the filling. Scatter with chopped hazelnuts and paint the borders of the galette with milk. Chill for 30 minutes.

7 Preheat the oven to 180°C fan (200°C/400°F/ Gas mark 6).

8 Bake the galette in the oven for 35–40 minutes until the pastry is golden and the filling is piping hot. Remove from the oven and dot blobs of Boursin over the filling. Sprinkle with the remaining tablespoon of tarragon and serve.

If you're not serving immediately, allow the galette to cool completely before covering and storing in the fridge for up to 2 days. To warm through, place on a baking sheet in the oven at 160°C fan (180°C/350°F/Gas mark 4) for 20–25 minutes until piping hot.

Roast garlic and lentil salad with caper dressing ⓥ

There aren't many salads that taste even better a day after you made them, but this batch-friendly summer recipe is a happy exception. It's a versatile dish that tastes sublime with the roast vegetables still warm from the oven but is just as good after a day or so. Lentil cooking times can vary, so follow your specific packet instructions to ensure they aren't overcooked.

FEEDS 4–6

1 whole bulb of garlic
400g/14oz shallots, peeled and cut
   lengthways into quarters
300g/10½oz cherry tomatoes
3 tbsp olive oil
300g/10½oz green or Puy lentils
100g/3½oz feta cheese or vegan alternative
30g/1oz basil leaves
salt and black pepper

FOR THE DRESSING
3 tbsp olive oil
1 red chilli, deseeded and roughly chopped
3 tbsp capers
grated zest and juice of 1 lemon
1 tbsp Dijon mustard

1 Preheat the oven to 180°C fan (200°C/400°F/ Gas mark 6).

2 Slice the base off the bottom of the garlic bulb. Tip the unpeeled garlic cloves, shallot quarters and cherry tomatoes into a roasting tin. Drizzle with the olive oil, season with salt and pepper and mix well to coat.

3 Roast in the oven for 40 minutes, stirring everything halfway through, until the vegetables begin to turn golden around the edges.

4 While they are roasting, cook the lentils according to the packet instructions. Drain and tip them into a deep serving bowl.

5 Remove the roasting tin from the oven and set aside the garlic cloves. Tip the shallots, tomatoes and any cooking juices into the bowl of lentils and mix gently.

6 Squeeze the roasted garlic cloves out of their skins into a mini food processor or small mixing bowl. Add the dressing ingredients and blitz or mash into a thick sauce. Season with salt and pepper. Drizzle the dressing over the lentils and gently fold through the salad.

7 Crumble the feta or vegan alternative over the salad and scatter with torn basil leaves before serving.

The salad will keep in an airtight container in the fridge for up to 2 days. Return to room temperature before serving.

Maple-glazed beetroot with walnuts and marjoram ⓥ

Sometimes you just look at a dish and find yourself smiling. This jolly jumble of sweet beetroot, tender shallots and marjoram is one of those. Marjoram isn't as popular as parsley or oregano, but here its lemony tartness is a perfect foil to the heady, dense sweetness of roasted beetroot. If you're making this in the summer, try and find multi-coloured or stripy beetroot. But don't worry if you can't, because this sweet dressing always lifts the spirits of chunkier, more workaday beetroot.

FEEDS 4

8 small beetroots, halved (or 4 large beetroots, quartered), peeled and scrubbed
8 banana shallots, peeled and trimmed, left whole
3 tbsp olive oil
5 marjoram or oregano sprigs
3 tbsp vegan-friendly sherry vinegar
1 tsp maple syrup
30g/1oz walnuts, chopped
salt and black pepper

1 Preheat the oven to 160°C fan (180°C/350°F/ Gas mark 4).

2 In a large, deep baking tray, toss the beetroots and shallots with the olive oil. Tuck in three of the marjoram or oregano sprigs, season with salt and pepper and roast in the oven for 1 hour, turning the beetroots and shallots halfway through the cooking time.

3 Remove the vegetables from the baking tray and keep warm. Discard the marjoram or oregano sprigs.

4 Place the tray over a medium heat and add the vinegar and maple syrup. Using a spatula, scrape up the pan juices and any vegetable bits and stir them together. Keep stirring over a low heat until the liquid starts to thicken and become syrupy.

5 Pour the syrupy juice over the warm vegetables, scatter the chopped walnuts over the top and sprinkle with marjoram or oregano leaves picked from the reserved sprigs.

6 Serve warm or at room temperature.

This recipe can be prepared without the walnuts up to 2 days in advance. If you are making it ahead, allow the vegetables to cool completely before covering and storing in the fridge. Bring back to room temperature and scatter with chopped walnuts before serving.

Green ribbon and bulgur wheat salad with lemon dressing ⓥ

A delicately light and simple salad full of glorious summer colours and flavours that can handily be made up to a day ahead. Keep the salad and dressing separate until you are ready to serve.

FEEDS 4

FOR THE DRESSING
finely grated zest of 1 lemon,
    plus 2 tbsp juice
6 tbsp olive oil
1 tsp Dijon mustard
2 tbsp capers, chopped
salt and black pepper

FOR THE SALAD
200g/7oz bulgur wheat
300ml/10fl oz boiling water
20g/¾oz chives, finely chopped
50g/1¾oz young spinach leaves, thinly sliced
20g/¾oz flat-leaf parsley leaves, finely chopped
4 tbsp toasted pine nuts
1 yellow pepper, deseeded and diced
1 green pepper, deseeded and diced
salt and black pepper

1 To make the dressing, mix the ingredients in a bowl and season to taste with salt and pepper. If you are making the salad in advance, cover the dressing and chill.

2 Place the bulgur wheat in a shallow heatproof bowl, cover with the boiling water and cover with cling film or a reusable plastic cover (I use a plastic shower cap!). Leave for 15 minutes, then remove the covering and fork through the bulgur wheat.

3 Add the remaining salad ingredients and mix well.

4 If you are eating immediately, pour the dressing over the salad, mix well and serve.

To make ahead, allow the salad to cool completely and keep in the fridge for up to 24 hours. Add the dressing just before serving.

Broccoli, lemon and almond salad Ⓥ

You will never be able to make enough of this warm salad, because it's so good that it disappears as soon as it hits the table. It works with everything from barbecues to Sunday roasts and is so easy to make that it's almost not even a recipe. I guarantee it will very quickly become a firm favourite. Make a double batch of the recipe and keep the extra in the fridge, ready to add to stir fries and breakfast fry-ups.

FEEDS 4

2 large heads of broccoli
grated zest and juice of 1 lemon
4 tbsp olive oil
30g/1oz flaked almonds, toasted
salt and black pepper

1   Trim the broccoli heads and cut into bite-sized pieces, including the stalk.

2   Bring a large pan of salted water to the boil and cook the broccoli for 4 minutes.

3   Drain the broccoli and tip it onto a large platter. Squeeze the lemon juice over the top and drizzle with the olive oil. Season generously with salt and pepper and scatter with the lemon zest and flaked almonds.

3 | Everyday feasts

When life is busy and demanding, feeding yourself and your household can sometimes feel like being on a treadmill. Mealtimes loom endlessly and it can be hard to find the motivation or energy to be creative with your everyday cooking.

The solution is to get your batch on! This chapter is full of friendly, accessible, everyday dishes that are guaranteed to welcome you home at the end of a long day. You won't find any grey mince, boring sludge or anaemic pies here, just noisy, energetic dishes that can be made ahead and stored, ready to bounce into life when you need them.

Set aside a little time to fill your fridge and freezer with meals that can be served up immediately, cooked in advance or prepared and frozen for days when you're pushed for time. From quick vegetable tarts that look as if they've been put together in a French patisserie to aromatic pulses and simple pastas, why shouldn't you be feasting every day?

Everyday feasts

Charred hispi cabbage with butter bean stew ⓥ

Harissa-glazed cauliflower, fennel and wild garlic bake ⓥ

Rocket, watercress and ricotta gnudi

Easy pea and spinach tart ⓥ

Smoky lettuce patties with sunrise salsa

Light chickpea and new potato curry ⓥ

Carrot, halloumi and mint fritters

Honey-roast fennel and shallots with creamy mustard mash ⓥ

Miso-chilli glazed aubergines with sesame noodle salad ⓥ

Spiced sweet potato oven chips ⓥ

Roasted double tomato tart ⓥ

Cumin-spiced lentils with crispy red cabbage ⓥ

Cannellini bean, sage and crispy tomato pasta ⓥ

Vibrant spring green, dill and pistachio orzo ⓥ

Black bean balls with mint and cucumber dip ⓥ

DIY pizza party (with freezable dough) ⓥ

Red pepper and mixed seed bulgur wheat salad ⓥ

Charred hispi cabbage with butter bean stew Ⓥ

Hispi cabbage, also known as sweetheart cabbage, has a wonderfully silky texture when it is baked, and by caramelising the cut sides first, you will end up with sweet crunchy edges too. Here, the cabbage wedges are charred, then cooked in a rich, aromatic butter bean stew topped with crunchy breadcrumbs and salty cheese. This can be prepared up to 24 hours before baking.

FEEDS 4 GENEROUSLY

4 tbsp olive oil
2 fat garlic cloves, crushed
2 small red onions, finely chopped
2 celery sticks, finely chopped
1 tsp dried oregano
large pinch of ground cinnamon
1 tsp smoked paprika
2 bay leaves
½ tsp sugar
2 tbsp tomato purée
2 x 400g/14oz tins chopped tomatoes
2 x 400g/14oz tins butter beans, drained
1 sweetheart/hispi cabbage
50g/1¾oz breadcrumbs
100g/3½oz feta cheese or vegan alternative, crumbled
salt and black pepper
2 tbsp chopped flat-leaf parsley, to serve

1 Heat half the oil in a large, deep frying pan over a medium heat, tip in the garlic, onions and celery and cook for 8–10 minutes until softened. Add the oregano, cinnamon, smoked paprika, bay leaves and sugar, and cook for a further 2 minutes.

   Stir in the tomato purée, chopped tomatoes and a tin of water, and season generously with salt and pepper. Bring to the boil, then reduce the heat and simmer for 5 minutes. Add the butter beans and bring back up to a simmer.

2 Tip the stew into an ovenproof casserole dish about 20 x 30cm (8 x 12in).

3 Preheat the oven to 160°C fan (180°C/350°F/ Gas mark 4).

4 Cut the cabbage into quarters lengthways, including the stem (which will help to hold the wedges together). Wipe the frying pan clean with paper towel, then heat the remaining olive oil in the pan over a medium-high heat and place the wedges cut side down in the pan. Cook for 5–6 minutes on each side, until slightly charred.

5 When the wedges are nicely charred, nestle them, cut side up, into the stew. Press breadcrumbs over the exposed edges.

6 Crumble the feta (or a vegan alternative) over the top and bake in the oven for 50–55 minutes until the stew is bubbling and the breadcrumbs are golden. If the top starts to burn, cover the pan loosely with a sheet of foil.

7 Remove the dish from the oven, scatter with parsley and serve.

Any leftovers make a fantastic fry-up, especially when topped with fried eggs or mushrooms. Thinly slice the cabbage and fry over a high heat. Warm the leftover beans in a small saucepan and top with the cabbage and eggs or mushrooms cooked your way.

Harissa-glazed cauliflower, fennel and wild garlic bake ⓥ

An easy one-tin bake, bursting with North African flavours, which is great as a main course with rice or grains, or as a filling for baked potatoes. Chop and fry any leftovers and top with roast tomatoes or a fried egg for a quick and feisty brunch. If wild garlic isn't in season, you can also use fresh coriander.

FEEDS 4 (EASILY DOUBLED)

1 large cauliflower
2 large fennel bulbs, thinly sliced
30g/1oz wild garlic leaves or fresh coriander, finely chopped
3 tbsp harissa
3 tbsp maple syrup
3 tbsp olive oil
grated zest and juice of 1 lemon
salt and black pepper

1 Preheat the oven to 160°C fan (180°C/350°F/ Gas mark 4).

2 Trim the cauliflower and cut it into 2cm (¾in)-thick slices as if it were a loaf of bread. Place the slices in a large roasting tray. Break any loose florets into small pieces and scatter them around the slices.

3 Add the fennel and half of the wild garlic or coriander. Season with salt and pepper.

4 Mix the harissa, maple syrup and olive oil in a bowl, then pour it over the vegetables. Toss everything together so that everything is evenly coated with the mixture. Roast in the oven for 40–45 minutes, turning the vegetables gently halfway through the cooking time until the cauliflower is tender and golden, but not mushy.

5 Remove from the oven and toss with the lemon zest and juice. Scatter with the remaining chopped wild garlic or coriander and serve.

Allow to cool completely before storing any leftovers in the fridge for up to 2 days.

Rocket, watercress and ricotta gnudi

Please try this recipe, it's so good! Gnudi are cute little flavour bombs, a bit like gnocchi but made without potato. The gnudi mixture will keep for up to 24 hours in the fridge, so I usually make lots, and keep half for the next day. You can also make the gnudi in advance, cover and reheat them in the oven later. I've also used the gnudi mixture as a potsticker filling, to an enthusiastic reception. The gnudi is served with grated cheese here, but you can also drizzle carrot-top pesto (p.71) or wild garlic pesto (p.166) over the top if you have any spare.

FEEDS 4

200g/7oz watercress
200g/7oz spinach
100g/3½oz rocket
250g/9oz ricotta
3 eggs
100g/3½oz extra-mature cheddar, grated,
     plus extra for serving
150g/5½oz plain flour
olive oil, for drizzling
grated zest of 1 lemon
30g/1oz basil leaves
salt and black pepper

1   Pour a kettle-full of boiling water slowly over the watercress, spinach and rocket in a colander for 1–2 minutes until it wilts. Cool in cold water, then squeeze the leaves with your hands or press them into the colander until you have drained the excess water and it feels dry.

2   Place the watercress, spinach, rocket, ricotta, eggs and 80g/2¾oz of the grated cheddar into a food processor and blitz for 2–3 seconds until it has the texture of a rough paste. Tip it into a large mixing bowl.

3   Add ½ teaspoon of salt and a generous quantity of black pepper, then add the flour and process again for a few seconds.

4   Spoon the mixture into a bowl, cover and chill for 30 minutes (or up to 24 hours).

5   When you are ready to cook, warm a large dish and drizzle with olive oil.

6   You will need to cook the gnudi in batches. Bring a large, shallow saucepan of water to the boil. When it is boiling, scoop 8–10 dessert-spoons of the chilled gnudi mixture out of the bowl and drop them into the boiling water. I find it easiest to use another spoon to scrape the mixture off the spoon and into the pan.

7   When the gnudis pop up to the surface, let them cook for 1 minute, then remove using a slotted spoon. Drain and slide them into the oiled dish. Keep warm while you use up the rest of the mixture.

8   To serve, sprinkle with the reserved cheddar and the lemon zest. Tear the basil leaves and scatter over the top. Season with salt and pepper and drizzle with oil. Serve immediately or cover with foil and set aside.

To warm the gnudi, if making them in advance, place the covered dish in a pre-heated oven at 160°C fan (180°C/350°F/Gas mark 4) for 30 minutes or until piping hot.

Easy pea and spinach tart (V)

This is one of my favourite recipes. It's wonderful in summer or winter, and despite being extremely easy to make, it looks as if you've gone to a great deal of effort. It's packed with vibrant colours and textures and tastes fabulous hot or cold. Credit for the vegan variation goes to a young friend, Daisy, who is an excellent baker.

FEEDS 4–6

1 sheet of ready-rolled all-butter or
    vegan puff pastry
40g/1½oz butter or 3 tbsp olive oil
1 onion, finely chopped
2 garlic cloves, finely chopped
2 eggs, beaten, or 1 flax egg*
350g/12oz frozen whole-leaf spinach, defrosted,
    drained and roughly chopped
150g/5½oz frozen peas, defrosted
5 tbsp oat cream (for the vegan variation only)
100g/3½oz feta, crumbled (or vegan alternative)
2 tbsp mixed seeds
a little milk or oat milk, for brushing
salt and black pepper

1 Preheat the oven to 180°C fan (200°C/400°F/ Gas mark 6).

2 Unroll the puff pastry and place it, still on its sheet of greaseproof paper, onto a large baking tray.

3 Score a line 1cm (½in) from the edge all the way around the pastry sheet, without cutting all the way through. This will rise during the initial bake and hold your filling in place. Prick the centre of the pastry sheet with a fork (within the scored border) and bake in the oven for 15 minutes while you get on with making the filling. Remove from the oven and set aside.

4 Heat the butter or olive oil in a small frying pan over a medium heat, add the onion and garlic and sauté gently for 6–8 minutes until softened, then set aside to cool for a few minutes.

5 Add the eggs (or flax egg) to a large bowl and stir in the chopped spinach and peas. If you are making the vegan version, stir in the oat cream.

6 Stir in the cooled onion and garlic and season generously with plenty of salt and pepper.

7 Spoon the vegetable mixture onto the pastry sheet, taking care to make sure it stays within the scored lines. Gently level the mixture so it's all roughly the same height.

8 Scatter with the crumbled feta (or vegan alternative) and top with mixed seeds, then brush the edges of the tart with a little milk.

9 Bake in the oven for 20–25 minutes, until the edges are golden brown. Remove from the oven and serve hot or cold. The cooled tart will keep in the fridge for 2 days.

* Mix 1 tablespoon of ground flax seed and 3 tablespoons of boiling water in a bowl. Leave to stand for 5 minutes.

Smoky lettuce patties with sunrise salsa

The idea of making burgers out of lettuce might sound unusual, but these flavoursome patties made from crisp iceberg lettuce, cheese and smoky spices are a revelation. They are good with a fresh salsa on the side or stacked in a burger bun with all the usual burger trimmings. You can make the patties a few hours in advance and keep them covered in the fridge before cooking.

FEEDS 4

300g/10½oz iceberg lettuce
60g/2¼oz mature cheddar, finely grated
150g/5½oz fine breadcrumbs
1 tsp smoked paprika
1 egg, beaten
½ tsp dried oregano
1 carrot, finely grated
4 tbsp plain flour
olive oil, for frying
salt and black pepper

FOR THE SALSA

3 different-coloured large tomatoes,
    finely chopped
½ small red onion, finely chopped
1 tbsp olive oil
handful of basil leaves, torn

1 Chop the lettuce very finely by hand or pulse in a food processor for 2 seconds, just until it is roughly minced and the size of large breadcrumbs.

2 Mix all the burger ingredients except the oil in a large bowl and season generously with salt and pepper. Form the mixture into 8 large patties (I use plastic gloves as the mixture is quite sticky) and place them on a baking sheet lined with greaseproof paper or a reusable liner. Cover and chill for at least 1 hour and up to 24 hours.

3 To cook, heat a little oil in a large non-stick frying pan over a medium-high heat. When the pan is hot, gently slide in half of the patties and press them down gently to flatten. Fry for 6–8 minutes until golden, then carefully flip and cook for the same time on the other side.

4 When they are ready, remove and keep warm while you cook the rest of the batch.

5 To make the salsa, mix all the ingredients together in a bowl and season with salt and pepper.

Light chickpea and new potato curry ⓥ

This mild curry, packed with velvety chickpeas, waxy new potatoes and whole spices, makes a flavour-packed lunch or a light supper. The ingredients list looks long but it's easy to make and keeps well in the fridge for a few days. Serve with rice, naan bread and your favourite pickles and chutneys.

FEEDS 4

2 tbsp vegetable oil
2 tsp cumin seeds
2 tsp yellow mustard seeds
2 onions, finely chopped
3 garlic cloves, crushed
20g/¾oz fresh ginger, peeled and grated
1 fresh red chilli, deseeded and finely chopped
1 tsp ground coriander
1 tsp ground cumin
½ tsp turmeric
750g/1lb 10oz baby potatoes, cut into
    3cm (1¼in) chunks
2 x 400g/14oz tins chopped tomatoes
300ml/10fl oz vegetable stock
1 x 400g/14oz tin chickpeas, drained
100g/3½oz fresh baby spinach
20g/¾oz coriander, chopped
salt and black pepper

1 Heat the vegetable oil in a large, deep frying pan over a medium-high heat. Add the cumin and mustard seeds and cook for a few seconds until they start to pop.

2 Reduce the heat, add the chopped onions and cook for 6–8 minutes until softened, then add the garlic, ginger and chilli and cook for 2 minutes. Sprinkle the dried spices over the onions, season with salt and pepper and cook for 2 minutes, stirring continuously.

3 Add the potatoes, chopped tomatoes and stock and bring to the boil. Reduce the heat and simmer for 15–20 minutes until the potatoes are cooked through. Add the chickpeas and cook until piping hot, then stir in the spinach for a few seconds until it starts to wilt.

4 Season with salt and pepper to taste, scatter with chopped coriander and serve.

Allow to cool completely and store in the fridge in an airtight container for up to 2 days. Reheat slowly until piping hot.

Carrot, halloumi and mint fritters

These minty gluten-free fritters are a great way of using up sad carrots lingering at the bottom of the fridge or leftover cooked carrots from a Sunday roast. If you're more in the mood for a burger, make them bigger and increase the cooking time to ensure they are cooked through.

MAKES 16 SMALL FRITTERS OR
8 BURGER PATTIES

400g/14oz carrots, peeled, trimmed and
  halved lengthways
4 tbsp olive oil, plus optional extra for frying
225g/8oz halloumi cheese, grated
1 small red onion, grated
100g/3½oz gluten-free fine breadcrumbs
2 eggs, beaten
4 tbsp gram flour, plus extra for dusting
10g/¼oz dill fronds, finely chopped
10g/¼oz mint leaves, finely chopped
salt and black pepper

1 Bring a pan of water to the boil. Drop the carrots into the pan and boil for 10 minutes.

2 Drain the carrots then, when they are cool enough to handle, coarsely grate them into a medium mixing bowl. Add 2 tablespoons of the oil and all the remaining ingredients and season well with salt and pepper. Mix well and chill for 1 hour.

3 Line a baking tray or platter with greaseproof paper or a reusable liner. Shape the carrot mixture into either 16 small fritters or 8 more substantial burger patties and lay them on the paper. Dust lightly with gram flour.

4 When you are ready to cook, heat the remaining 2 tablespoons of olive oil in a large non-stick frying pan over a medium heat. When the oil is hot, cook the fritters or burgers in batches for 4–5 minutes on each side until crisp and golden (adding more oil to the pan if necessary).

The fritter mixture can be made up to 24 hours in advance and chilled.

Honey-roast fennel and shallots with creamy mustard mash ⓥ

Honey and mustard is a classic flavour combination that works beautifully in everything from salads to marinades. This sweet and sticky fennel with smooth and silky mash is rich and filling and, speaking from experience, no matter how much you make it will never be enough.

FEEDS 6–8

8 fennel bulbs, tops trimmed off and
    feathery fronds reserved
800g/1lb 12oz large echalion shallots,
    peeled and halved lengthways
2 tbsp olive oil
80g/2¾oz butter or vegan margarine
4 tbsp runny honey or maple syrup
grated zest and juice of 2 lemons
salt and black pepper

FOR THE MUSTARD MASH

1.5kg/3lb 5oz floury potatoes, peeled
    and cut into chunks
100–120ml/3½–4fl oz whole milk,
    almond milk or oat milk
2 tbsp butter or olive oil
2 tbsp wholegrain mustard

1   To prepare the fennel, cut the trimmed bulbs in half lengthways. Trim the base but don't remove the core as it will hold the fennel together while you caramelise the cut sides.

2   You will need to cook the fennel and shallots in batches. Heat the oil and butter (or margarine) in a large, deep frying pan over a medium heat. Place 4 fennel halves in the pan, cut side down, and cook for 10–12 minutes until the cut sides are golden. Try not to move the pieces and do not turn them over. Remove the fennel with a slotted spoon and place, cut side up, in a large roasting tin or ovenproof casserole dish. Repeat with the remaining fennel halves.

3   Repeat the process with the shallots and tuck them in, also cut side up, around the fennel. Pour any juices left in the frying pan over the top.

4   Preheat the oven to 180°C fan (200°C/400°F/ Gas mark 6).

5   Mix the honey (or maple syrup) and lemon juice together and drizzle over the vegetables. Season well with salt and pepper. Cover with foil and bake in the oven for 45–50 minutes until the fennel is cooked through, removing the foil halfway through the cooking time.

6 While it's baking, make the mustard mash. Cook the potatoes in boiling water for 12–15 minutes until cooked through and tender. Drain, then mash as smoothly as you can (use a potato ricer if you have one). Add the milk, butter (or oil) and mustard. Season generously to taste with salt and pepper.

7 To serve, dollop a generous pile of mash onto each plate and top with the roasted fennel and shallots. Drizzle any cooking juices over the top. Finely chop the reserved fennel fronds and scatter them over the top, along with the lemon zest.

Cool completely before storing the roasted vegetables and mash separately in airtight containers in the fridge for up to 2 days. Reheat the mash until piping hot. Slice leftover fennel and/or shallots and add it to stews, soups or breakfast hashes.

Miso-chilli glazed aubergines with sesame noodle salad ⓥ

This useful dish works equally well as a cold noodle salad or as a piping hot stir-fry, so you can happily keep the leftovers in the fridge for hungry moments. It can be difficult to get stir-fry sauces to properly coat the protein or vegetable elements of a dish, but this rich and clingy sauce does it brilliantly.

FEEDS 4

3 aubergines, trimmed and each cut
    lengthways into 6 pieces
4 tbsp sunflower oil
2 tbsp vegan-friendly sherry
1 tbsp light soy sauce
1 red chilli, deseeded and finely chopped
20g/¾oz fresh ginger, peeled and grated
2 garlic cloves, crushed
2 tsp cornflour
1 tbsp sesame oil
150ml/5fl oz vegetable stock
1 tbsp red miso paste
250g/9oz soba noodles
small bunch of spring onions, finely chopped
20g/¾oz coriander leaves, chopped

FOR THE SESAME DRESSING
2 tbsp mixed black and white sesame seeds
2 tbsp sesame oil
2 tbsp light soy sauce

1 Cut each piece of aubergine widthways into 4 pieces so each aubergine yields 24 chunks.

2 In a large bowl, toss the aubergine in the sunflower oil.

3 You will need to cook the aubergine in batches. Heat a large, deep frying pan over a medium heat and place a single layer of aubergine pieces over the base. Fry for 6–8 minutes over a medium-high heat, turning the pieces occasionally until they are golden. Transfer to a warm plate and repeat until all the aubergine pieces are cooked.

4 Whisk the sherry with the light soy sauce, chilli, ginger, garlic, cornflour and sesame oil. Add the stock and 100ml/3½fl oz water and mix well.

5 Pour the sauce into the same pan you cooked the aubergine in and bring to the boil. Reduce the heat and simmer the sauce until it has reduced by about half and is rich and thick. Add the miso paste and stir until it has dissolved in the sauce. Tip in the cooked aubergines and warm through, stirring until they are slickly coated with sauce. Keep warm.

6 To make the sesame dressing, mix the sesame seeds, sesame oil and soy sauce in a small bowl. Cook the noodles according to the packet instructions, drain and toss with the sesame dressing (you may find this easier to do with your hands) and place in a large serving bowl.

7 Top the noodles with the aubergines and sauce and scatter with the spring onions and coriander. Serve immediately.

If you are making this dish in advance to eat as a salad, allow to cool completely (without the coriander and spring onions). Cover and keep in the fridge for up to 24 hours. Bring back to room temperature, add the coriander and spring onions and toss well before serving.

Spiced sweet potato oven chips Ⓥ

Making your own oven chips is quick and easy. They only need a little preparation, so it's worth making a few batches for the freezer, ready for when you're tired and in need of comforting carbs.

FEEDS 4 AS A SIDE DISH

4 large sweet potatoes, peeled
4–6 tbsp olive oil
1½ tsp smoked paprika
½ tsp cayenne pepper
salt and black pepper

1 Cut the potatoes into long chip-shaped pieces, about 1cm (½in) wide. Rinse and drain the chips.

2 Bring a large pan of water to the boil.

3 Fill a large bowl with cold water and add a few ice cubes.

4 Place half the drained chips into the boiling water and boil for 2 minutes. Drain and tip into the iced water. When they are cool, drain and spread them out onto a clean, dry tea towel. Gently shake and pat them dry. Repeat the process with the remaining chips.

5 Put 3 tablespoons of the olive oil and the spices in a large mixing bowl. Season with salt and pepper and mix well.

6 Tip in the chips and mix until they are evenly coated in the oil. You might need to do this in batches, adding a little more of the oil if needed.

7 To cook, preheat the oven to 180°C fan (200°C/400°F/Gas mark 6) and lightly grease a large baking tray. Shake the chips out onto the tray, spread them out in an even layer and bake in the oven for 30–35 minutes, turning them halfway through the cooking time, until the chips are crisp and piping hot inside.

To freeze the uncooked chips, tip them into large, reusable freezer bags. Lay the freezer bags flat and arrange the chips in a single layer. Empty the air out of the bags and seal. Place the bags flat in the freezer as this makes it easier to shake out and separate the chips on a baking tray when you are ready to cook. Cook the chips from frozen as above, but extend the cooking time to 40–45 minutes.

Roasted double tomato tart ⓥ

Here's another super-easy tart with deceptively deep, summery flavours. The tart can be made ahead, so it's perfect for grabbing a slice from the fridge when you're on the run, or baking a few batches in advance if you're cooking ahead for a crowd. The top is all about drama, colour and texture, with vibrantly sunny red and orange hues. Hiding underneath is a rich filling threaded with flavour blasts from sun-dried tomatoes, lemon and basil.

FEEDS 4–6

1 sheet of ready-rolled all-butter or
    vegan puff pastry
250g/9oz ricotta or vegan alternative
grated zest of 1 lemon
2 tsp Dijon mustard
5 sun-dried tomatoes in oil, drained and
    finely chopped
30g/1oz basil leaves, torn into small pieces
2 big beef tomatoes, about 400g/14oz
    (different colours if you can find them)
100g/3½oz mixed yellow, orange and
    red cherry tomatoes
3 tbsp oil from the jar of sun-dried tomatoes
salt and black pepper

1 Preheat the oven to 180°C fan (200°C/400°F/ Gas mark 6).

2 Unroll the puff pastry and place it, still on its sheet of greaseproof paper, onto a large baking tray. Score a line 1cm (½in) from the edge all the way around the sheet without cutting through. Prick the pastry all over with a fork inside the scored line.

3 Bake the pastry in the oven for 15 minutes, until the border has puffed up and the base is lightly golden, then remove and set aside for a few minutes to cool.

4 Mix the ricotta (or vegan alternative), lemon zest, mustard, sun-dried tomatoes, and half of the torn basil leaves in a small bowl. Season generously with salt and pepper.

5 Spread the ricotta mixture evenly inside the borders of the baked pastry sheet.

6 Slice the beef tomatoes thickly and arrange them randomly across the ricotta mixture. Cut the cherry tomatoes in half horizontally and tuck them between the tomato slices.

7 Drizzle the tart with the sun-dried tomato oil, season again and roast in the oven for 25–30 minutes until the tomatoes are starting to caramelise and the pastry is golden.

8 Remove from the oven, and if you are serving the tart immediately, scatter with the remaining basil and serve. If you are making ahead, allow to cool completely, before storing in the fridge for up to 24 hours. Bring back to room temperature and sprinkle with basil before serving.

Cumin-spiced lentils with crispy red cabbage ⓥ

A hearty, healthy vegan recipe that makes a big vat of colourful warming lentils and crispy red cabbage. Either scatter the cabbage on top of the lentils or swirl them together to create one big, multi-coloured pot of joy. Rice or naan breads would be a good accompaniment if you're making it for a big meal, but a bowl and a spoon is all that's required if you're in need of a quick pit-stop. This was originally inspired by a much-loved Madhur Jaffrey recipe and a desire to use up half a leftover red cabbage, but it's now firmly ensconced as one of our family favourites.

FEEDS 6–8

2 tsp yellow mustard seeds
2 tsp cumin seeds
4 tbsp sunflower oil
3 garlic cloves, crushed
40g/1½oz fresh ginger, peeled and grated
1 red chilli, deseeded and finely chopped
1 tsp ground cumin
½ tsp ground turmeric
300g/10½oz red lentils, rinsed and drained
2 x 400g/14oz tins chopped tomatoes
2 tsp sugar
2 red onions, halved and thinly sliced
large bunch of coriander, leaves stripped, stalks finely chopped
400g/14oz trimmed red cabbage, thinly sliced
2 limes, cut into wedges
salt and black pepper

1   Place a large, heavy-based saucepan over a medium-high heat, add the mustard and cumin seeds and dry-fry for 1 minute until they start to pop. Add 2 tablespoons of the oil and the garlic, ginger, chilli, ground cumin and turmeric and cook for 2 minutes.

2   Add the lentils, tomatoes, sugar, 1 teaspoon of salt, a generous grind of pepper and 1 litre/34fl oz of water. Bring to the boil, then reduce the heat and simmer for 40–50 minutes until the lentils are soft and soupy. Taste and add more salt if needed.

3   While the lentils are cooking, heat the remaining oil in a large frying pan over a medium heat, add the sliced onions and coriander stalks and cook for 6–8 minutes until softened, then add the sliced cabbage. Increase the heat to medium-high and cook for 12–15 minutes until the cabbage is cooked and slightly crispy around the edges. Season to taste with salt and pepper.

4   Mix the cabbage mixture into the lentils and warm through. Serve with the lime wedges and a generous scattering of coriander leaves.

To freeze, cool completely and store in an airtight container for up to 2 months. Defrost completely before reheating slowly until piping hot.

Cannellini bean, sage and crispy tomato pasta Ⓥ

This is a quick, creamy and satisfyingly clingy sauce that can be thrown together while you're waiting for your pasta to cook. Sage and crispy sun-dried tomato shreds add sweet, citrusy tones and crunchy textures. Save time by making two or three extra batches for the freezer.

FEEDS 4

2 x 400g/14oz tins cannellini beans, drained
16 sun-dried tomatoes in oil
6 tbsp oil from the jar of sun-dried tomatoes
grated zest and juice of 1 lemon
4 shallots, halved and thinly sliced
2 garlic cloves, finely chopped
8 sage leaves, thinly sliced
400g/14oz dried spaghetti
4 tbsp chopped flat-leaf parsley
50g/1¾oz mature cheddar or vegan alternative, finely grated
salt and black pepper

1 Place the drained beans into the bowl of a food processor and add 8 of the sun-dried tomatoes and 3 tablespoons of the oil. Add 2 tablespoons of lemon juice and 2 tablespoons of water and blitz to a purée, then scrape out into a bowl.

2 Heat 2 tablespoons of the sun-dried tomato oil in a frying pan over a medium heat, add the shallots, garlic and sage and cook for 8–10 minutes until softened and lightly golden.

3 Spoon the shallot mixture into the bean purée. Taste and add more lemon juice if needed. Season generously with salt and pepper and keep warm.

4 Thinly slice the remaining sun-dried tomatoes. Add the last tablespoon of oil to the frying pan and fry the sliced tomatoes over a high heat until crispy. Set aside.

5 Bring a large pan of salted water to the boil and cook the spaghetti according to the packet instructions. Before draining, remove 200ml/7fl oz of the pasta cooking water and add it to the sauce.

6 Drain the pasta and toss with the sauce.

7 Scatter the lemon zest, crispy sun-dried tomatoes, chopped parsley and cheddar (or vegan alternative) over the pasta and serve immediately.

The sauce will keep in the fridge for up to 2 days, or in an airtight container in the freezer for up to 2 months. Cool completely before chilling or freezing. To reheat, add 2–4 tablespoons of water to loosen the sauce and warm slowly until piping hot.

Vibrant spring green, dill and pistachio orzo Ⓥ

This quick orzo dish is full of green vegetables and fresh lemony dill. It can be served piping hot, or as a salad at room temperature. Either way, it's green and gorgeous and positively brimming with the joys of spring and summer.

FEEDS 4

2 tbsp olive oil
2 leeks, thinly sliced
2 garlic cloves, finely chopped
2 celery sticks, thinly sliced
large bunch of dill, fronds picked,
    stalks finely chopped
300g/10½oz spring greens, finely shredded
300g/10½oz orzo
700ml/24fl oz warm vegetable stock
150g/5½oz frozen peas, defrosted
150g/5½oz baby spinach leaves
200g/7oz feta or vegan alternative, crumbled
grated zest and juice of 2 lemons
salt and black pepper
70g/2½oz unsalted pistachios, toasted and
    chopped, to serve
2 tbsp toasted pine nuts

1   Heat the oil in a large, deep frying pan over a medium heat, add the leeks, garlic, celery, chopped dill stalks and a good pinch of salt and cook for 6–8 minutes until softened.

2   Add the spring greens and cook for another 4 minutes, then tip in the orzo and stir for 2 minutes until it is coated in the oil.

3   Pour half of the stock into the pan and stir until it is absorbed, then add the remaining stock and bring to the boil. Reduce the heat, cover and simmer gently for 8–10 minutes until the orzo is cooked.

4   Add the peas and spinach leaves and stir gently until the spinach leaves have wilted.

5   Remove from the heat and stir in the lemon zest and juice, and crumbled feta (or vegan alternative). Season generously with salt and pepper.

6   Roughly chop the dill fronds and scatter them over the orzo. Mix in the chopped pistachios and sprinkle with pine nuts before serving.

To chill, allow to cool completely and store in the fridge for up to 2 days. Bring back to room temperature and fluff with a fork before serving, to separate the orzo.

Black bean balls with mint and cucumber dip ⓥ

These balls bury the notion that pulse-based meatball alternatives are stodgy, by virtue of being frisky little herb and spice-packed balls of joy. We always make a double batch as they freeze well and work brilliantly for lunch, supper or just as snacks. My top tip is to use plastic gloves when you're rolling the bean balls, so the mixture doesn't stick to your hands.

MAKES 25–30 BEAN BALLS

2 tbsp olive oil, plus extra for cooking
1 onion, finely chopped
4 garlic cloves, finely chopped
2 red chillies, deseeded and finely chopped
30g/1oz basil, stalks finely chopped, leaves set aside
1 tsp dried oregano
½ tsp ground cumin
1 tsp smoked paprika
2 x 400g/14oz tins black beans, drained
6 tbsp tomato purée
120g/4oz fine breadcrumbs
40g/1½oz extra-mature cheddar or vegan alternative, finely grated
2 eggs, beaten, or 2 flax eggs*
salt and black pepper

FOR THE MINT AND CUCUMBER DIP

150g/5½oz Greek yoghurt or vegan alternative
15g/½oz mint leaves, finely chopped
½ cucumber, finely chopped

*
Mix 2 tablespoons of ground flax seed with 6 tablespoons of boiling water in a bowl. Leave to stand for 5 minutes.

1   Heat the 2 tablespoons of olive oil in a frying pan over a medium heat, add the onion, garlic, chillies and basil stalks with a pinch of salt and fry for 6–8 minutes until softened. Add the dried oregano, cumin and paprika and cook for another 2 minutes. Set aside.

2   Tip the drained beans into a bowl and mash until they are slightly broken and have a rough, chunky texture. Add the onion mixture and stir well.

3   Set aside a handful of basil leaves and tear the rest into the beans. Add the tomato purée, breadcrumbs, grated cheddar (or vegan alternative) and the eggs (or flax eggs) to the bowl. Season generously with salt and pepper and mix well.

4   Line a baking tray with greaseproof paper or a reusable liner.

5   Take a walnut-sized amount of the bean mixture and roll it as lightly as you can between your palms into a small ball. Place it on the baking tray and repeat until the mixture is finished – you should have 25–30 balls. Place the tray in the fridge for 30 minutes (or up to 24 hours).

➤➤➤

6   While the balls are firming up, mix the
    yoghurt (or vegan alternative), chopped mint
    and cucumber in a small bowl. Season with
    salt and pepper.

7   To cook the bean balls, heat 2 tablespoons
    of olive oil in a large non-stick frying pan
    over a medium-high heat and add 8–10 balls.
    Cook for 6–8 minutes, turning the balls
    occasionally, until cooked through and nicely
    crisp on the outside. Remove from the pan
    and keep warm. Repeat with the remaining
    balls, adding more oil as necessary.

8   Scatter with the reserved basil leaves and
    serve warm, with the cucumber and mint
    sauce on the side.

    To freeze the uncooked balls, place the tray in
    the freezer and open freeze for 40 minutes to
    firm up. Tip into airtight bags or boxes. Cook
    as above from frozen for 10–12 minutes, until
    piping hot and cooked through.

DIY pizza party (with freezable dough) Ⓥ

Everyone loves a homemade pizza night, but it does take a little time to prepare. I usually make big batches of tomato sauce for the freezer, which just leaves the dough to make on the day. But when a friend told me she freezes her pizza dough too, I had to give it a try. Now we make batches of both for (almost) instant pizza nights.

FEEDS 4 (WITH EXTRA SAUCE FOR THE FREEZER)

FOR THE PIZZA SAUCE (FEEDS 8)
4 tbsp olive oil
1 large onion, finely chopped
4 garlic cloves, crushed
2 tbsp finely chopped fresh oregano leaves,
    or 2 tsp dried
3 x 400g/14oz tins chopped tomatoes
1 tsp sugar
salt and black pepper

FOR THE PIZZA DOUGH (FEEDS 4)
7g/¼oz dried quick/instant yeast
1½ tsp caster sugar
1½ tsp fine salt
1 tbsp olive oil, plus extra for greasing
320ml/11fl oz tepid water
600g/1lb 5oz strong white bread flour,
    plus extra for dusting

FOR THE TOPPING
4 balls of mozzarella or vegan alternative,
    torn into small pieces
2 large handfuls of basil leaves
olive oil, for drizzling
8 black or green olives, stoned and
    halved (optional)

1 First, make the pizza sauce. Heat the oil in a heavy-based saucepan over a medium heat, add the onion, garlic and oregano and fry gently for 8–10 minutes until softened. Add the chopped tomatoes and sugar and bring to the boil, then reduce the heat and simmer for 40 minutes until the sauce is rich and syrupy.

2 Remove from the heat and blitz the sauce with a stick blender or mash with a potato masher until smooth. Season well with salt and pepper and allow to cool. The sauce keeps for up to 3 days in the fridge and can be frozen for up to 1 month.

3 To make the pizza dough, mix the yeast, sugar, salt, olive oil and tepid water together in a bowl. Stir well and leave for 5 minutes.

4 Place the flour into a large mixing bowl and make a dip in the centre. Pour the yeast mixture into the dip and gradually mix until you have a shaggy dough. Turn the dough out onto a floured surface and knead for 10 minutes, until smooth and springy.

5 Clean the mixing bowl and grease it with a little oil. Place the dough back in the bowl, cover with greased cling film or a silicone lid, then set it aside to rise in a warm place until it has doubled in size (this will take about 1 hour).

6 When the dough has risen, divide it into 4 pieces and lightly brush them with oil. You can use the dough straight away or, if you are freezing the portions, gently wrap each one in cling film or reusable (freezable) wrapping, taking care not to squash them. Freeze for up to 1 month. Remove the dough portions from the freezer 3 hours before you are going to cook them, loosening the wrappings slightly so the dough can expand.

7 Preheat the oven to 200°C fan (220°C/425°F/ Gas mark 7).

8 On a floured surface, roll out each ball of dough to the size of a large dinner plate. Transfer to a floured baking sheet or pizza stone. Cover with a thin layer of tomato sauce and scatter over equal amounts of mozzarella (or a vegan alternative). Add the olives, if using.

9 Bake in the oven for 10–12 minutes, until the dough is lightly golden and the topping is bubbling. Remove from the oven, scatter with basil leaves, drizzle with olive oil and serve immediately.

Red pepper and mixed seed bulgur wheat salad (V)

Bulgur wheat is such a useful ingredient. It needs very little cooking and keeps well. Make a big batch of this colourful salad and serve it warm or at room temperature.

FEEDS 4 AS A MAIN COURSE OR 8 AS A SIDE

4 tbsp olive oil
3 red peppers, deseeded and cut into thin strips
1 large onion, halved and thinly sliced
3 garlic cloves, finely chopped
small bunch of flat-leaf parsley, stalks and
    leaves finely chopped separately
2 tbsp tomato purée
200g/7oz bulgur wheat
400ml/14fl oz vegetable stock
5 tbsp mixed seeds
grated zest and juice of 1 lemon
salt and black pepper

1 Heat the olive oil in a large, deep frying pan over a medium heat, add the peppers, onion, garlic and parsley stalks and cook for 10–12 minutes until softened, then add the tomato purée and bulgur wheat and stir for 1 minute. Season well with salt and pepper.

2 Pour the vegetable stock into the pan and stir. Cover the pan with a tight-fitting lid and reduce the heat to its lowest setting. Cook for 10 minutes without removing the lid.

3 Turn off the heat and leave to stand for another 10 minutes without uncovering.

4 Remove the lid and gently fluff the wheat with a fork to separate the grains. Stir in the mixed seeds, chopped parsley leaves, lemon zest and juice. Taste and add more seasoning if desired. Serve warm or at room temperature.

The salad can be made up to 2 days in advance. Allow to cool completely then store in the fridge. Return to room temperature before serving.

4 | Family-friendly big batches

J oining the party with a glass of wine while the cooker does the work is my favourite kind of meal. However, feeding a crowd has become a little more complicated: one of the joys of cooking for a tableful of hungry people used to be watching everyone come together and share a big, beautiful dish, but tastes and preferences are changing, and it can be a challenge to find family-sized meals that work for meat-eaters, vegetarians and vegans without lots of extra work for the cook.

So that's what this chapter is all about: big, blowsy recipes for make-ahead dishes to feed between six and eight people. It's a mixture of crowd-pleasing classics such as oozy lasagnes and stuffed vegetables, showstoppers like my vegan honeycomb cannelloni or roasted celeriac, as well as more humble dishes that are happy to snuggle up as part of a feast. I promise you that no one will feel short-changed, so you can get on and invite your favourite people without a second thought.

Most recipes can be easily halved if that suits you better, or you can make the full batch and feed yourself for more than a week! And if it doesn't all get eaten at the first sitting, most of the leftovers can be repurposed. Batch cooking really does come into its own when you're feeding a crowd.

Family-friendly big batches

Triple green lasagne

Mushroom, broccoli and walnut lasagne

Butternut, lemongrass and peanut stew ⓥ

Roast root veg pilaf ⓥ

Universal vegan base ⓥ

Honeycomb courgette cannelloni with a rye top ⓥ

Summer veg-patch risotto ⓥ

Sticky aubergine bao buns with smacked cucumber ⓥ

Roast celeriac with saffron and herb yoghurt ⓥ

Rich tomato, thyme and red pepper sauce ⓥ

Stuffed artichoke cups ⓥ

Sweet potatoes with zingy herb sauce ⓥ

Freekeh-stuffed courgettes with olives and marjoram ⓥ

Smoky chipotle and maple baked beans ⓥ

Wild garlic pesto with wholemeal spaghetti ⓥ

Triple green lasagne

There's nothing quite like a lasagne on a chilly winter night to bring joy and comfort. This is one of my favourite alternatives to traditional tomato-based lasagnes. It's a gloriously green bake, made with lots of cheese and a satisfying pine nut crunch. As with all lasagnes, it takes a little time to prepare, but you can save time by making the fillings or the whole dish in advance.

FEEDS 6—8

250g/9oz fresh kale, roughly chopped
130g/4½oz butter, plus extra for greasing
2 leeks, thinly sliced
500g/1lb 2oz spinach leaves
250g/9oz ricotta
40g/1½oz toasted pine nuts
grated zest of 1 lemon
80g/2¾oz plain flour
1 tsp English mustard powder
pinch of paprika
1 litre/34fl oz whole milk
200g/7oz mature cheddar, grated
250–300g/9oz–10½oz fresh lasagne sheets
salt and black pepper

1 Grease a deep 20 x 30cm (8 x 12in) ovenproof dish with butter.

2 Bring a large saucepan of water to the boil, add the kale and boil for 6 minutes. Drain and finely chop, especially any large stems, and return to the empty saucepan.

3 Melt 30g/1oz of the butter in a large frying pan over a medium heat and add the leeks and a pinch of salt. Sauté for 8–10 minutes until softened. Add the leeks to the cooked kale and season well.

4 Melt 20g/¾oz of the butter in the same frying pan and add the spinach. Cook for 2–3 minutes until it has wilted and there is no liquid left in the pan.

5 Drain and chop the spinach. Return it to the frying pan and stir in the ricotta, pine nuts and lemon zest. Season generously with salt and pepper and set aside.

6 Place the remaining 80g/2¾oz of butter, flour, mustard powder and paprika into a saucepan over a medium heat. Stir for 1 minute, until it becomes a golden paste, then gradually add the milk, stirring between each addition. Cook for 10–12 minutes until the sauce has thickened. Remove from the heat and season with salt and pepper.

7   Set aside 50g/1¾oz of the cheddar. Stir the remaining cheddar into the white sauce, then set aside 200ml/7fl oz of the sauce for the top of the lasagne. Pour the rest of the sauce into the kale mixture.

8   To assemble the lasagne, spread a third of the kale filling over the bottom of the dish. Cover with a layer of fresh pasta. Spoon half of the spinach filling evenly over the top and smooth. Spoon over another third of the kale filling and cover with another layer of pasta. Add the rest of the spinach, then a final layer of kale. Top with a third layer of pasta. Pour over the reserved cheese sauce and sprinkle with the remaining cheddar.

9   The lasagne can be covered and kept in the fridge for up to 24 hours before cooking.

10 Preheat the oven to 160°C fan (180°C/350°F/ Gas mark 4). Bake the lasagne in the oven for 50 minutes–1 hour, until piping hot and golden brown. Leftovers can be kept in the fridge for up to 2 days or frozen in portions.

To freeze the cooked lasagne, cool completely, wrap tightly in foil or reusable wrapping and freeze for up to 1 month. Defrost, remove the foil or wrapping and reheat at 160°C fan (180°C/350°F/Gas mark 4) for 35–45 minutes until piping hot.

Mushroom, broccoli and walnut lasagne

Lasagnes do take a little effort, and this is no exception, but it is a gratifyingly rich, creamy showstopper that will keep a big crowd of your special people very happy.
If you want to get ahead, you can make the lasagne or the fillings up to a day in advance.
The secret to the success of this dish is to ensure the mushrooms are golden and a little crispy around the edges.

FEEDS 8

4–5 tbsp olive oil
120g/4oz butter, plus extra for greasing
2 garlic cloves, crushed
400g/14oz leeks, sliced into thin medallions
1kg/2lb 4oz mixed mushrooms, thinly sliced
2 tbsp finely chopped thyme leaves
80g/2¾oz plain flour
1 tsp English mustard powder
pinch of paprika
1 litre/34fl oz whole milk
200g/7oz mature cheddar, grated
250–300g/9–10½oz fresh lasagne sheets
200g/7oz broccoli, cut into small
   bite-sized pieces
80g/2¾oz walnuts, chopped
100g/3½oz mozzarella, diced
salt and black pepper

1 Grease a deep 20 x 30cm (8 x 12in) ovenproof dish with butter.

2 Warm 2 tablespoons of the oil with 20g/¾oz of the butter in a large frying pan over a medium heat, add the garlic, leeks and a pinch of salt and sauté for 6–8 minutes until softened. Remove the leeks from the pan and set aside in a bowl.

3 Add another 20g/¾oz of the butter, a generous pinch of salt, half of the mushrooms and half the thyme leaves to the frying pan. Cook briskly over a high heat for 10–12 minutes until lightly golden. Tip the mushrooms into the leeks.

4 Add the remaining oil, mushrooms and thyme and another pinch of salt to the pan and cook the mushrooms for 10–12 minutes until golden, then add to the leek mixture.

5 Place the remaining 80g/2¾oz of butter, the flour, mustard powder and paprika into a saucepan. Heat and stir for 1 minute, until it becomes a golden paste, then gradually add the milk, stirring continuously. Cook for 10–12 minutes until the sauce has thickened. Remove from the heat and stir in the cheddar. Taste and season with salt and pepper.

6   Set aside 200ml/7fl oz of the cheese sauce for the top of the lasagne, then stir the chopped broccoli and walnuts into the remaining sauce.

7   To build the lasagne, spread half of the mushroom filling over the bottom of the dish. Cover with half of the broccoli sauce and a layer of lasagne sheets. Spoon the remaining mushroom filling on top and spread it evenly. Pour over the remaining broccoli sauce and cover with lasagne sheets. Spread the reserved cheese sauce evenly over the top. Scatter with diced mozzarella and add a generous grind of black pepper.

8   The lasagne can be covered and kept in the fridge for up to 24 hours before cooking.

9   Preheat the oven to 160°C fan (180°C/350°F/ Gas mark 4). Bake the lasagne in the oven for 50 minutes–1 hour until piping hot and golden brown. Leftovers can be kept in the fridge for up to 2 days or frozen in portions.

To freeze the cooked lasagne, let it cool completely, wrap tightly in foil or reusable wrapping and freeze for up to 1 month. Defrost, remove the foil or wrapping and reheat at 160°C fan (180°C/350°F/Gas mark 4) for 35–45 minutes until piping hot.

Butternut, lemongrass and peanut stew Ⓥ

This easy, warm and substantial delight of a dish goes well with rice, chutneys and fresh green spinach. Chunks of sweet, dense squash are perfectly balanced with salty peanuts. It's a perfect batch-cook to make in the autumn when squashes are cheap and plentiful. You can also substitute leftover Halloween pumpkins for butternut if you have some to hand.

FEEDS 8 AS PART OF A FEAST

4 lemongrass stalks, trimmed, split in half
    lengthways and finely chopped
1.5kg/3lb 5oz butternut squash, peeled, deseeded
    and chopped into 2cm (¾in) pieces
4 tbsp vegetable oil
1 x 400g/14oz tin chopped tomatoes
40g/1½oz fresh ginger, peeled and grated
3 garlic cloves, peeled
1½ tsp turmeric
2 red chillies, deseeded and roughly chopped
1 tbsp soft dark brown sugar
2 red onions, halved and thinly sliced
2 x 400g/14oz tins coconut milk
2 large red peppers, deseeded and thinly sliced
120g/4oz roasted salted peanuts
salt and black pepper
large handful of coriander leaves, to serve

1 Preheat the oven to 180°C fan (200°C/400°F/ Gas mark 6).

2 Place the chopped lemongrass into a small heatproof bowl and add 4 tablespoons of boiling water. Leave for 10 minutes to infuse.

3 Tip the chunks of butternut squash into a large roasting tin and drizzle with 2 tablespoons of the vegetable oil. Season with salt and pepper and toss to coat it with oil. Roast in the oven for 30 minutes, until the squash is tender and caramelised around the edges, turning the chunks halfway through.

4 While the butternut squash is roasting, tip the chopped tomatoes into a mini food processor. Add the lemongrass and soaking water, ginger, garlic, turmeric, chillies, sugar and 1 teaspoon of salt. Add a generous grind of black pepper and blitz to a wet paste.

5 Heat the remaining 2 tablespoons of vegetable oil in a large, heavy-based saucepan over a medium heat and add the sliced onions. Fry gently for 10–12 minutes until softened and just starting to turn golden, then pour in the tomato mix and add a tin of water.

6 Bring to the boil, then reduce the heat to a vigorous simmer and cook for 15 minutes.

7 When the butternut squash is cooked, add it to the tomato sauce. Stir in the coconut milk, red peppers and peanuts and cook for 8–10 minutes until the sauce is thick and rich and the squash is piping hot. Taste and add more seasoning if desired. If serving straight away, scatter with coriander.

The stew will keep in the fridge for up to 2 days. Reheat gently in a saucepan, stirring as little as possible and adding a few tablespoons of water to loosen the sauce if needed. Scatter with coriander to serve.

Roast root veg pilaf Ⓥ

This is an excellent way to use up any random root vegetables that are lurking in the bottom of your fridge. I usually include beetroot, carrots and butternut squash because of their sweetness and jewel-like colours, but it's also good with parsnips, sweet potatoes and celeriac.

FEEDS 8

2 parsnips, peeled and cut into 2cm (¾in) chunks
300g/10½oz peeled and deseeded butternut
    squash, cut into 2cm (¾in) chunks
4 carrots, peeled and cut into 1cm (½in) chunks
3 beetroots, scrubbed and cut into
    2cm (¾in) chunks
3 tsp cumin seeds
5 tbsp olive oil
2 red onions, finely chopped
2 yellow peppers, deseeded and cut
    into small strips
1 red chilli, deseeded and finely chopped
1 tbsp ground coriander
2 tsp ground cumin
2 tsp turmeric
½ tsp ground cardamom
2 cinnamon sticks
400g/14oz basmati rice, rinsed and drained
1 litre/34fl oz vegetable stock
juice of 1 lemon
40g/1½oz cashew nuts, roasted and chopped
large handful of flat-leaf parsley leaves, chopped
salt and black pepper

1. Preheat the oven to 180°C fan (200°C/400°F/ Gas mark 6).

2. Place the parsnips, butternut squash, carrots and beetroots on a baking tray. Scatter with cumin seeds and drizzle over 3 tablespoons of the olive oil. Season with salt and pepper and toss so the vegetables are evenly coated. Roast in the oven for 35–40 minutes until the vegetables are lightly golden around the edges, turning them halfway through the cooking time.

3. While the vegetables are roasting, heat the remaining olive oil in a large ovenproof casserole dish over a medium heat, add the onions, yellow peppers and chilli and cook for 8–10 minutes until the onions have softened.

4. Add all the spices and season generously with salt and pepper. Stir and cook for 2 minutes.

5. Add the rice and cook for 2 minutes, stirring until it is coated with the oil and spices.

6. Add the stock, stir, then bring to the boil. Stir again, cover with a tight-fitting lid and place in the oven for 20–25 minutes.

7. When the rice is cooked, fluff it up with a fork, squeeze the lemon juice over the top, stir in the cashew nuts and adjust the seasoning if desired.

8. Top with the roasted vegetables and any cooking juices, then scatter with parsley and serve.

The pilaf will keep in the fridge for up to 3 days. Allow to cool completely before storing. Bring back to room temperature to serve cold, or reheat until piping hot.

Universal vegan base ⓥ

This is one of the recipes I cook most often, but to be honest, I didn't know what to call it. It is essentially a hugely versatile, tomatoey sauce that you can literally eat straight from the pan, or use as a base for pasta, chilli, pies, stuffed vegetables or winter stews.

There is a fair amount of chopping involved, but the reward is a massive quantity of sauce which freezes beautifully. In the testing stage of this recipe, we made enough to feed 48, which kept everyone happily fed for weeks! One tip: the veggies reduce in size, but the lentils do the opposite, so you'll need a nice big pan. Lentil cooking times can vary, so keep a close eye on yours to ensure they don't overcook and become mushy.

MAKES 12 PORTIONS

4 tbsp oil from a jar of sun-dried tomatoes in oil
2 fennel bulbs, diced into 5mm (¼in) pieces
1 large red onion, finely chopped
2 carrots, finely chopped
3 celery sticks, finely chopped
2 leeks, sliced into thin medallions
4 garlic cloves, crushed
3 tsp dried oregano
500g/1lb 2oz dried green or Puy lentils
4 tbsp tomato purée
12 sun-dried tomatoes in oil, finely chopped
4 x 400g/14oz tins chopped tomatoes
salt and black pepper

1 Place the sun-dried tomato oil, fennel, onion, carrots, celery, leeks, garlic, oregano, and a big pinch of salt into a large, heavy-based pan and place over a medium heat. Sauté gently for 20 minutes, until the vegetables have softened without browning.

2 Add the lentils, tomato purée, chopped sun-dried tomatoes, chopped tomatoes, four tins of water and 1 teaspoon of salt. Stir well, partially cover, and bring to the boil. When it is boiling, reduce the heat and simmer vigorously for 45–55 minutes until the sauce is rich and thick and the lentils are cooked. Taste and add more salt and pepper if desired.

To freeze, allow to cool completely and place in airtight containers or sealed bags for up to 3 months. Defrost completely before reheating slowly until piping hot.

Honeycomb courgette cannelloni with a rye top ⓥ

This was a mad idea that began as a quick dish for a friend who couldn't find a good vegan cannelloni recipe, but it turned out to be a bit of a showstopper. The rich, tomato-based filling wrapped in silky courgette coils is all topped with a crunchy herb and garlic crumb. If you can find different coloured courgettes, so much the better.

FEEDS 8

2–3 large courgettes (about 500g/1lb 2oz), trimmed
½ batch of Universal Vegan Base (p.144)
30g/1oz butter or vegan alternative, plus extra for greasing
120g/4oz rye or brown fine breadcrumbs
2 garlic cloves, crushed
3 tbsp finely chopped chives
3 tbsp rapeseed or olive oil
grated zest of 1 lemon
50g/1¾oz mature cheddar or vegan alternative, finely grated
salt and black pepper

1 Slice the courgettes thinly lengthways using a Y-shaped vegetable peeler or mandoline.

2 Place the slices in a large bowl, sprinkle with 2 teaspoons of salt and mix gently without breaking them. Leave for 15 minutes, rinse, then carefully pat dry with a clean tea towel.

3 Grease a 20 x 30cm (8 x 12in) ovenproof dish with butter (or vegan alternative).

4 To assemble the cannelloni, take a courgette slice and roll it up into a short tube, leaving a space the size of your thumb in the centre. Fill the centre with the lentil mixture and place the courgette tube upright in the dish. Repeat with the remaining courgette slices and fillings until the dish is full of tightly packed, filled courgette tubes.

5 In a small bowl, mix the breadcrumbs, garlic, chives, oil and lemon zest. Season with salt and pepper. Spoon the breadcrumbs evenly over the top of the courgette cannelloni and scatter with the grated cheddar (or vegan alternative).

6 The prepared dish can be kept in the fridge for up to 24 hours before baking.

7 Preheat the oven to 160°C fan (180°C/350°F/ Gas mark 4). Bake in the oven for 50 minutes–1 hour until bubbling, golden and piping hot.

Summer veg-patch risotto

This is a happy risotto, full of the tastes and colours of summer. It's best made with firm baby courgettes, and if you can find both the yellow and green versions, it will look even better. It needs nothing more on the side than a big fresh green salad with a lemony dressing to continue the colour theme and invigorate the taste buds.

FEEDS 8

5 tbsp olive oil
500g/1lb 2oz baby courgettes, halved lengthways and thinly sliced
4 garlic cloves, finely chopped
1.5–1.75 litres/2½–3 pints vegetable stock
1 large onion, finely chopped
2 celery sticks, finely chopped
20g/¾oz flat-leaf parsley, stalks finely chopped, leaves set aside
2 tsp dried oregano
600g/1lb 5oz risotto rice
80ml/2¾fl oz white wine
250g/9oz fresh or frozen broad beans
200g/7oz fresh or frozen peas
150g/5½oz extra-mature cheddar or vegan alternative, finely grated
grated zest and juice of 1 lemon
salt and black pepper

1 Heat 2 tablespoons of the olive oil in a large, heavy-based pan over a medium-high heat. Add the sliced courgettes, garlic and a generous pinch of salt and cook for 6–8 minutes until lightly golden. Remove the courgettes from the pan with a slotted spatula and set aside.

2 Heat the stock in a separate saucepan.

3 Add the remaining oil to the large pan, reduce the heat to medium, and add the onion, celery, parsley stalks and oregano. Stir and cook for 3–4 minutes until translucent, without letting them brown. Add the risotto rice and cook for another 3 minutes, stirring frequently.

4 Pour in the white wine and stir until it has been absorbed, then add the hot stock to the rice a ladleful at a time, stirring between each addition, until the liquid has been absorbed. This will take 20–30 minutes, so make sure you have a glass of your favourite beverage to hand to help you with the process. When you have added 1.5 litres/2½ pints of stock, taste the rice to see if it is cooked. It should have a slightly nutty, but not crunchy texture. If it is still too firm, continue adding more stock, gradually, until the rice is ready. Cool and save any excess stock to add to soups or stews.

5   While the risotto is cooking, bring a pan of
    water to the boil. Add the broad beans and
    cook for 1 minute. Add the peas and turn off
    the heat. Leave for 2 minutes, then drain and
    tip into cold water. Remove and discard the
    grey outer skin of the broad beans.

6   When the rice is cooked, add the courgettes,
    beans and peas and heat through.

7   Stir in the grated cheddar (or vegan
    alternative), lemon zest and juice. Taste
    and season with salt and pepper as required.
    If you are serving the risotto straight away,
    chop the parsley leaves and scatter them over
    the risotto.

    To freeze, allow to cool completely and store in
    airtight containers. Add 6 tablespoons of
    boiling water or stock to loosen the risotto
    and reheat gently until piping hot. Scatter
    with parsley leaves and serve.

Sticky aubergine bao buns with smacked cucumber ⓥ

Bao buns and kits are readily available, and making your own fillings is quick and easy. This vegan filling is made with aubergine coated in a potent, salty-sweet sauce and it's my absolute favourite. Pile the aubergine up high in your bao buns and top it with a heap of fiery smacked cucumber. Both can be made up to a day in advance.

MAKES ENOUGH FOR 16 BAO BUNS

FOR THE SMACKED CUCUMBER
1 cucumber, trimmed and halved lengthways,
    seeds removed with a spoon
4 tbsp rice vinegar
2 tbsp caster sugar
1 red chilli, finely chopped
1 tsp Maldon salt

FOR THE STICKY AUBERGINE BAO BUNS
4 tbsp light soy sauce
4 tbsp smooth peanut butter
2 tbsp runny honey or maple syrup
1 tbsp red miso paste
1 tbsp sesame oil
1 tbsp rice vinegar
2 garlic cloves, crushed
4 aubergines (about 1kg/2lb 4oz),
    cut into 1cm (½in) cubes
120ml/4fl oz rapeseed oil
3 tbsp white sesame seeds
16 ready-made bao buns
2 bunches of spring onions, cut into matchsticks
small bunch of coriander, leaves picked

1 To make the smacked cucumber, slice the cucumber halves widthways into thin half-moon shapes. Whisk the rice vinegar, caster sugar, chilli and salt in a bowl and add the cucumber. Toss the cucumber in the dressing, cover and keep in the fridge for up to 24 hours.

2 To make the aubergine sauce, put the soy sauce, peanut butter, honey or maple syrup, miso paste, sesame oil, rice vinegar and crushed garlic into a small food processor or bowl. Blitz or whisk to a thin sauce and set aside.

3 Tip the cubed aubergine into a large bowl and add the rapeseed oil. Toss with your hands until the aubergine is evenly coated.

4 Heat a large frying pan over a high heat and add a third of the aubergine. Fry for 6–8 minutes, turning and pressing lightly on the chunks until they are golden all over. Tip onto a plate and repeat with the remaining aubergine.

5 Return all the aubergine to the pan, add the sauce and stir gently to coat the aubergine, without squashing the chunks. Heat until piping hot and add 2 tablespoons of the sesame seeds.

6 To serve, place a few spoonfuls of the sticky aubergine into each bao bun. Sprinkle the remaining sesame seeds, spring onions and coriander over the top. Serve with the smacked cucumber salad.

The aubergine sauce will keep in the fridge for up to 24 hours. Heat until piping hot before serving.

Roast celeriac with saffron and herb yoghurt ⓥ

This spectacular-looking dish takes a while to cook, but the oven does all the hard work. The yoghurt sauces can be thrown together at the last moment, so you can do something else while the celeriac is getting on with the business of becoming delicious. Leftovers can be chopped into small chunks and mixed with couscous or bulgur wheat, or added to a breakfast hash.

FEEDS 8 AS PART OF A FEAST

2 large celeriac (about 900g/2lb each)
5 tbsp olive oil
2 tsp Maldon salt
4 tsp ras-el-hanout spice blend
4 tbsp pomegranate seeds (optional), to serve

FOR THE SAFFRON AND HERB YOGHURTS
30g/1oz dill fronds, finely chopped
30g/1oz mint leaves, finely chopped
large pinch of saffron threads
1 tbsp boiling water
600g/1lb 5oz plain Greek yoghurt or
    vegan alternative
salt and black pepper

1 Preheat the oven to 170°C fan (190°C/375°F/ Gas mark 5).

2 Wash and trim the celeriac but do not peel them. Pierce them all over with a fork (at least 10 times each). The skin can be quite tough, so I find it easiest to do this with a quick stabbing action. Place the celeriac into a large roasting tin.

3 Mix the olive oil, salt and ras-el-hanout spice blend in a small bowl. Using your hands, smother the mixture all over the celeriac.

4 Place in the oven and roast for 2–2½ hours, basting the celeriac roughly every 40 minutes or so until the celeriac is dark brown, tender and gently oozing when pricked with a knife. Towards the end of the cooking time, make the sauce.

5 Set a tablespoon each of chopped dill and mint aside for the finished dish.

6 Place the saffron threads in a small heatproof bowl and cover with the boiling water. Leave to infuse for 10 minutes.

7 Put half the yoghurt (or vegan alternative) into a bowl and strain the saffron soaking liquid over the top. Mix well.

8 In a separate bowl, mix the remaining chopped herbs with the rest of the yoghurt (or vegan alternative). Season well with salt and pepper.

9 When the celeriac is ready, cut them each horizontally into 8 thick steaks and carefully turn these over in the pan juices. Keep warm until you are ready to eat

10 Serve the steaks drizzled with both sauces and scatter with the reserved fresh herbs and pomegranate seeds (if using)

Leftovers should be allowed to cool completely, then can be stored in the fridge for up to 2 days.

Rich tomato, thyme and red pepper sauce Ⓥ

This silky, fire engine-red pasta sauce uses just a few ingredients and requires very little preparation, thanks mostly to jarred red peppers – one of my favourite store-cupboard ingredients. Their slightly tart flavour is balanced by a rich tomato and garlic base. I like to toss the sauce with pasta curls or twists, but it's equally good with spaghetti or linguine.

FEEDS 8

12 thyme sprigs, leaves picked
5 tbsp olive oil
3 x 400g/14oz tins chopped tomatoes
4 garlic cloves, peeled and finely chopped
good pinch of dried chilli flakes
1 tbsp honey or maple syrup
1 x 450g/1lb jar cooked red peppers, drained and rinsed, and drained again
6 tbsp double cream or almond cream
600g/1lb 5oz dried pasta
4 tbsp grated mature cheddar or vegan alternative
salt and black pepper
2 tbsp finely chopped parsley (optional)

1 Place the thyme leaves, olive oil, chopped tomatoes, garlic, chilli and a tin of water into a heavy-based saucepan. Season well with salt and pepper. Bring to the boil, then reduce the heat and simmer for 30–40 minutes, stirring regularly, until the sauce is thick and large bubbles start popping up. Turn off the heat and stir in the honey or maple syrup. Allow to cool slightly.

2 Put the drained peppers into a food processor and blitz for a few seconds. Add the tomato sauce and blitz again until the mixture has a smooth dropping consistency.

3 Taste and add more salt and pepper if desired. Add the cream and keep warm.

4 Bring a large pan of salted water to the boil and cook the pasta according to the packet instructions. Drain the pasta, then stir in the sauce. Serve sprinkled with chopped parsley and grated cheese (or vegan alternative).

The sauce can be kept in the fridge for up to 3 days. To freeze, cool completely and store for up to 1 month in an airtight container. Defrost completely and reheat gently until piping hot.

Stuffed artichoke cups ⓥ

There's nothing quite like an edible plate, which is why stuffed artichoke bases are so good. These are stuffed with nuts, soft dill and tart capers. You can buy the cooked artichoke bases either frozen or tinned.

FEEDS 8 AS A STARTER OR AS PART OF A FEAST

1 tbsp olive oil, plus extra for drizzling
8 cooked artichoke bottoms, rinsed
    and drained
1 leek, thinly sliced
2 celery sticks, finely chopped
1 garlic clove, crushed
100g/3½oz fine breadcrumbs
15g/½oz dill fronds, finely chopped
30g/1oz toasted flaked almonds
3 tbsp capers, drained and finely chopped
100g/3½oz tomatoes, diced
100g/3½oz goats' cheese or vegan alternative,
    roughly chopped
salt and black pepper

1 Preheat the oven to 160°C fan (180°C/350°F/ Gas mark 4).

2 Drizzle a little oil over the base of a baking tin that is large enough to fit all the artichoke bases snugly. Place the artichoke bases in the tin.

3 Heat the tablespoon of olive oil in a small frying pan over a medium heat, add the leek, celery and garlic with a good pinch of salt and cook for 6–8 minutes until softened but not browned. Set aside.

4 Reserve 3 tablespoons of breadcrumbs, 1 tablespoon of the chopped dill fronds and 1 tablespoon of the flaked almonds. Mix the remaining breadcrumbs, dill and almonds together in a bowl, add the capers, tomatoes and goats' cheese (or vegan alternative) and season well.

5 Spoon equal amounts of stuffing into the artichoke bases and top with the reserved breadcrumbs. Drizzle with a little oil.

6 Bake in the oven for 25–30 minutes until golden brown and cooked through.

7 Serve warm, sprinkled with the reserved dill and almonds.

The bases can be prepared up to 24 hours before roasting and kept covered in the fridge.

Sweet potatoes with zingy herb sauce ⓥ

You are never far from an easy meal if you have a potato to hand, which is probably why they've featured heavily in my cooking repertoire since my student days. Baked sweet potatoes come into their own when paired with tart flavours that balance their intense sweetness. The potatoes and sauce in this recipe can be baked and prepared up to a day ahead, so all you need to do is reheat and get drizzling. You can also make the sauce without yoghurt, which gives it a much punchier citrus flavour and a bright green hue.

FEEDS 8

8 sweet potatoes, scrubbed
6 tbsp olive oil, plus extra for greasing
30g/1oz coriander leaves
6 spring onions
1 green chilli, deseeded
grated zest and juice of 1 lime
15g/½oz mint leaves
150g/5½oz Greek yoghurt or vegan alternative
50g/1¾oz roasted salted peanuts, chopped
salt and black pepper

1 Preheat the oven to 180°C fan (200°C/400°F/ Gas mark 6).

2 Place the potatoes on a greased baking tray and pierce them several times with a skewer. Drizzle over 2 tablespoons of the olive oil and roll them around to coat them in the oil. Season liberally with salt and pepper and bake in the oven for 40–50 minutes until tender.

3 Set aside a few coriander leaves for serving, then place the rest in a small food processor with the remaining olive oil, spring onions, chilli, lime zest and juice, mint leaves and yoghurt (or vegan alternative). Season with salt and pepper and blitz for a few seconds until smooth.

4 To serve, cut a cross in each cooked potato and dollop over generous spoonfuls of sauce. Scatter with the reserved coriander and chopped peanuts.

You can cook the potatoes a day in advance. Cook the potatoes then cool completely and store in the fridge for 24 hours. Reheat until piping hot. The sauce can also be made up to 24 hours in advance and stored in the fridge.

Freekeh-stuffed courgettes with olives and marjoram ⓥ

The key to making stuffed vegetables sing is to throw plenty of flavour at them. Here, they are filled with summery Mediterranean ingredients and freekeh cooked with aromatics and stock. Freekeh is an ancient grain with a nutty texture which also makes a great alternative to risotto rice.

FEEDS 8

150g/5½oz freekeh
2 bay leaves
1 tbsp tomato purée
600ml/20fl oz vegetable stock
8 courgettes, halved lengthways
50g/1¾oz olives, stoned and quartered
10 sun-dried tomatoes in oil, drained
    and finely chopped
2 tbsp oil from the sun-dried tomatoes jar,
    plus extra for drizzling
grated zest and juice of 1 lemon
1 tbsp finely chopped marjoram or oregano leaves
3 tbsp toasted pine nuts
30g/1oz fine breadcrumbs
salt and black pepper

1   Place the freekeh in a saucepan with the bay leaves, tomato purée and stock. Season with salt and pepper and bring to the boil. Reduce the heat to a simmer, partially cover and cook for 40–45 minutes until the freekeh is cooked through.

2   Bring a large pan of salted water to the boil.

3   Remove the courgette seeds with a spoon, without cutting through the base of the skin.

4   When the water is boiling, drop the courgette halves in and cook for 3 minutes. Drain and pat dry with a tea towel. Place on a large, greased baking tray.

5   To make the stuffing, mix the olives, chopped sun-dried tomatoes, 2 tablespoons of sun-dried tomato oil, lemon zest and juice, marjoram or oregano leaves and pine nuts in a bowl.

6   Preheat the oven to 200°C fan (220°C/425°F/ Gas mark 7).

7   When the freekeh is ready, stir it into the stuffing ingredients. Stuff the courgettes with the filling and sprinkle with the breadcrumbs. Drizzle with oil.

8   Roast the courgettes in the oven for 20–25 minutes until golden brown and piping hot.

The cooled courgettes will keep in the fridge for up to 24 hours. If you are cooking in advance, bring the courgettes back to room temperature before serving.

Smoky chipotle and
maple baked beans Ⓥ

Once you've made these, I promise there will be no going back to traditional tinned baked beans! This punchy recipe infuses beans with a deep, smoky warmth. It's a family-sized dish that is great on baked potatoes, toast or as part of a feast, and, of course, any leftovers should be sent straight to the breakfast table. You can replace the tinned beans here with red kidney beans or butter beans if desired.

FEEDS 8

4 tbsp oil from a jar of sun-dried tomatoes in oil
15g/½oz flat-leaf parsley, stalks finely chopped, leaves set aside
2 celery sticks, thinly sliced
2 onions, halved and thinly sliced
3 garlic cloves, crushed
1 tsp smoked sweet paprika
2 tsp chipotle paste
2 bay leaves
1 tbsp cider vinegar
2 tbsp chopped fresh marjoram or oregano
6 sun-dried tomatoes in oil, finely chopped
1 tbsp maple syrup
2 x 400g/14oz tins chopped tomatoes
1 x 400g/14oz tin cannellini beans
1 x 400g/14oz tin borlotti beans
1 x 400g/14oz tin mixed beans
salt and black pepper

1   Heat the oil in a large, heavy-based saucepan over a medium heat. Add the parsley stalks, celery, onions and a pinch of salt and cook for 8–10 minutes until softened but not browned. Add the garlic and cook for another 2 minutes. Sprinkle in the smoked paprika, add the chipotle paste and bay leaves and stir for 2 minutes. Add the vinegar and stir for 1 minute.

2   Add the remaining ingredients and a tin of water, season well with salt and pepper and bring to the boil. Reduce the heat to a vigorous simmer and cook uncovered for 30–35 minutes, stirring regularly, until the sauce has reduced and is rich and syrupy. Season to taste with plenty of salt and pepper.

3   Finely chop the parsley leaves and scatter them over the beans before serving.

The cooled beans will keep for up to 3 days in an airtight container in the fridge.

Wild garlic pesto with wholemeal spaghetti Ⓥ

Wild garlic is one of those few ingredients whose availability is strictly seasonal, which makes it even more precious when the young leaves come through in late spring. It has a gorgeous fresh flavour, which is milder than bulb garlic, but if you prefer your pesto a little less potent, replace half of the garlic leaves in the recipe with fresh basil.

FEEDS 8

200g/7oz young wild garlic leaves, roughly chopped
160g/5½oz extra-mature cheddar or vegan alternative, finely grated
200ml/7fl oz olive oil, plus extra for drizzling
80g/2¾oz toasted pine nuts
600–800g/1lb 5oz–1lb 12oz dried wholemeal spaghetti
salt and black pepper

1   Put the wild garlic in a food processor with the grated cheddar (or vegan alternative) and half of the olive oil. Process until it forms a rough paste. Add a little more oil and process again until it will just drop off the end of a spoon. Add a generous amount of black pepper and taste, then add a little salt if needed. Transfer to a bowl and stir in the pine nuts. Drizzle a little olive oil over the top of the pesto to help preserve colour.

2   When you are ready to eat, bring a large pan of salted water to the boil and cook the spaghetti according to the packet instructions. Drain and toss in the pesto. Serve with extra cheddar (or vegan alternative) if you prefer a more intense flavour.

The pesto will keep for up to 3 days in a covered container in the fridge.

5 | Sweets and treats

Baking sweet things always feels like a treat for the cook as well as the recipients. When else can you surround yourself and everyone in your household with sweetly scented clouds of cinnamon and vanilla while enjoying the anticipation of sugary delights and happy people?

My first experience of batch baking was making gingerbread hearts with my mother. We baked the hearts and threaded them onto red ribbons before storing them carefully between layers of greaseproof paper to hand out at primary school the next day. I've been hooked on baking ever since.

This chapter is my ruthlessly edited shortlist of tried-and-tested bakes that work for every occasion. If you're looking for a quick and easy grown-up cake or pudding, crunchy biscuits to cheer up a friend in need, or a monster-sized traybake for a crowd with a big appetite, you'll find it here. There are freezable doughs, cakes and loaves, and recipes that you can split to satisfy your sweet cravings now and later.

When you bake, there's usually enough to share, which is handy as these batch bakes make wonderful presents. There is nothing that lifts the spirits like homemade cakes or biscuits delivered or posted to the people you care about most. Happy baking!

Sweets and treats

Maple, oat and marzipan biscuits ⓥ

Lime and thyme shortbread thins

Pistachio and cherry brownies

Red plum and marzipan tartlets ⓥ

Cornflake florentines ⓥ

Blood orange upside-down cake

Feed-a-crowd crunchy apple traybake

Carrot and raisin loaves

Blueberry and lemon drizzle cake

Huge chocolate and orange traybake

Jumbleberry sorbet ⓥ

Cherry, coconut and banana loaf ⓥ

Lemon and elderflower slices

Jewelled pear and ginger cake

Maple, oat and marzipan biscuits ⓥ

These might look like flapjacks, but they are oh, so much better! Light, crunchy and sweet, they take just a few minutes to make and will helpfully stay crisp for several days. This recipe is a great way to use up leftover chunks of Easter or Christmas marzipan, but if you're not a fan, they are just as good without.

MAKES 24 LITTLE BISCUITS

90g/3oz butter or vegan margarine
1 tbsp maple syrup
80g/2¾oz golden caster sugar
½ tsp bicarbonate of soda
200g/7oz porridge oats
60g/2¼oz plain flour
50g/1¾oz marzipan, diced

1   Preheat the oven to 160°C fan (180°C/350°F/ Gas mark 4) and line a large baking sheet with greaseproof paper or a reusable non-stick liner.

2   Warm the butter or margarine, maple syrup and sugar together in a saucepan over a low heat until the butter has melted. Turn off the heat.

3   Dissolve the bicarbonate of soda in a table-spoon of boiling water, then add it to the butter mixture and stir well. The mixture will froth and bubble a little.

4   Add the oats, flour and diced marzipan and stir until completely combined. It might seem dry, but eventually the mixture will come together.

5   Dollop 24 heaped tablespoons of the mixture onto the lined baking sheet, spacing them out evenly.

6   Bake in the oven for 18–20 minutes, until golden. Remove from the oven and allow to cool and firm up for 5 minutes. Transfer to a cooling rack.

The biscuits will keep in an airtight container at room temperature for up to 3 days.

Lime and thyme shortbread thins

These meltingly light shortbread thins somehow manage to taste rich, fresh and citrusy all at the same time, and as a result they are completely addictive. This big-batch recipe makes a mountain of biscuits, so I usually freeze half of the dough, but you can also halve the quantity if you prefer.

MAKES 80 SMALL BISCUITS

250g/9oz butter, softened
150g/5½oz caster sugar
grated zest of 4 limes
350g/12oz plain flour, plus extra for dusting
2 egg yolks
50g/1¾oz cornflour
3 tbsp chopped thyme leaves
1–2 tbsp lime juice
150g/5½oz icing sugar

1   Preheat the oven to 160°C fan (180°C/350°F/ Gas mark 4) and line two large baking trays with greaseproof paper or reusable non-stick liners.

2   Beat the butter and sugar together in a bowl with a wooden spoon (or with an electric mixer) until pale and fluffy. Add the lime zest, plain flour, egg yolks, cornflour and 2 table-spoons of the chopped thyme leaves. Mix until it forms a shaggy dough.

3   Lightly dust a work surface with flour and tip the dough out onto it. Using your hands, shape the dough roughly into a ball. If you are planning to freeze half of the dough, wrap it in cling film or reusable (freezable) wrapping and freeze it now.

4   Roll the dough out to a thickness of 3mm (⅛in) and cut out 5–6cm (2–2½in) circles.

5   Place the circles on the lined baking trays. Gather the dough trimmings, re-roll and continue to cut out more circles until you have used all the dough (40 circles of dough if you have used half the dough, 80 if you have used it all).

6   Prick the biscuits with a fork and bake in the oven for 12–14 minutes until the edges are golden. Remove from the oven and leave on their baking trays for 5 minutes before transferring to a cooling rack.

7   When the biscuits have cooled, mix the lime juice with the icing sugar in a bowl to a smooth dropping consistency. Spread half a teaspoon of icing on top of each cooled biscuit and sprinkle with the remaining chopped thyme leaves.

The biscuits can be stored in an airtight container for up to 3 days.

To cook the dough from frozen, allow the dough to defrost, then follow the baking and icing instructions above.

Pistachio and cherry brownies

It was impossible not to include a brownie recipe in this book. They are the most requested sweet treats in my house and every new variety is devoured with enthusiasm. I tend to use a mixture of dark and milk chocolate, so they aren't too sweet or too bitter. Brownies don't have to be made with expensive chocolate; they will taste just as good made with whatever is to hand. Cherry and pistachio is one of my favourite sweet combinations and the gorgeous jewel-like colours are a bonus. If you happen to have a jar of alcohol-infused cherries, they make a deliciously boozy version: just drain and stone before using. I like to use a heart-shaped cutter for these indulgent brownies, which has the bonus of producing some handy offcuts for the cook, but you can also cut them into traditional squares.

MAKES ABOUT 16 BROWNIES

175g/6oz butter
100g/3½oz dark chocolate, broken into pieces
100g/3½oz milk chocolate, broken into pieces
320g/11¼oz caster sugar
50g/1¾oz dried cherries, halved
3 eggs, beaten
150g/5½oz plain flour
50g/1¾oz unsalted pistachio nuts, chopped

1 Preheat the oven to 150°C fan (170°C/340°F/ Gas mark 3) and line the base and sides of a square baking tin (about 20–23cm/8–9in) with greaseproof paper or a reusable non-stick liner.

2 Bring a saucepan half-filled with water to the boil, then reduce the heat to a simmer. Place the butter and chocolate in a large heatproof glass bowl, place over the water, making sure the bottom of the bowl doesn't touch the water, and stir the chocolate and butter together as they melt.

3 Remove the bowl from the heat and immediately stir in the sugar and cherries, then the beaten eggs, followed by the flour.

4 Tip the mixture into the lined tin, spread it out evenly and scatter the chopped pistachio nuts over the top. Bake in the oven for 45–50 minutes, until it has set but still has a slight wobble. Place the tin on a cooling rack and allow to cool completely before cutting into 16 squares, or use any shaped cookie cutter to create your preferred portions.

The brownies will keep in an airtight container in the fridge for up to 5 days.

The cooked, cut brownies can be frozen in layers, separated by greaseproof paper or reusable liners for up to 1 month. Defrost before serving.

Red plum and marzipan tartlets ⓥ

These cute little tartlets look as if they should be in the window of a French patisserie, but they're incredibly easy to make and use only five ingredients. They can be made in advance and frozen.

MAKES 8 TARTLETS

1 sheet of ready-rolled butter or
    vegan puff pastry
100g/3½oz marzipan, coarsely grated
300g/10½oz deep red or black plums,
    stoned and thinly sliced
1 egg, beaten, or 2 tbsp almond milk
3 tbsp sieved apricot jam

1 Preheat the oven to 200°C fan (220°C/425°F/ Gas mark 7) and line a large baking sheet with greaseproof paper or a reusable non-stick liner.

2 Unroll the puff pastry sheet and place it on the lined baking sheet. Cut it into 8 equal-sized rectangles and separate them slightly. Score a line 5mm (¼in) from the edges of each rectangle without cutting all the way through. The edges will puff up and make a border to contain the fillings. Use a fork to press little lines around the borders of each rectangle. Sprinkle grated marzipan evenly inside the borders.

3 Lay the sliced plums on top of the grated marzipan on each tart, again avoiding the borders.

4 Brush the borders of each tartlet case with beaten egg or almond milk and bake in the oven for 20–25 minutes until nicely golden underneath and around the edges. Remove from the oven and place on a cooling rack.

5 Mix the apricot jam with 1 teaspoon of water and warm it for a few seconds in a microwave or the heat of the oven until runny.

6 Paint the jam over the tartlets with a pastry brush.

To freeze, allow to cool completely and place between layers of greaseproof paper in an airtight bag or container. Freeze for up to 2 months and defrost completely before serving.

Cornflake florentines (V)

Three generations of my family have made chocolate cornflake cakes for birthday parties, but this recipe takes the idea to a new, grown-up level. I've used pecans and sour cherries here, but it works equally well with peanuts and raisins. Be warned, it is a messy, splattery business so if you have any mini chefs around, do get them involved, as they'll love it! These will keep for up to a week in an airtight tin, but I'd lay money on the fact that they won't last more than a day.

MAKES 25–30 FLORENTINES

120g/4oz cornflakes
100g/3½oz pecans, roughly chopped
50g/1¾oz cashews, roughly chopped
75g/2¾oz dried sour cherries, halved
1 x 397g/14oz tin dairy or vegan condensed milk
250g/9oz dark chocolate, broken into small pieces

1 Preheat the oven to 170°C fan (190°C/375°F/ Gas mark 5) and line two large baking trays with greaseproof paper or reusable non-stick liners.

2 Mix all the ingredients except the chocolate in a large mixing bowl. Place heaped tablespoons of the mixture, spaced a few centimetres apart, onto the two trays.

3 Bake in the oven for 10–12 minutes until golden brown. Leave to cool for 10 minutes, then peel off the paper or liners and place the florentines flat side up on cooling racks.

4 Bring a small pan of water to the boil, then reduce the heat to a simmer. Put the chocolate in a heatproof bowl and place the bowl over the saucepan, making sure the bowl doesn't touch the water. Stir until the chocolate has melted, then remove from the heat.

5 Paint the base of each florentine with melted chocolate and return to the cooling rack, chocolate side up. Chill until the chocolate has set.

The florentines can be stored in an airtight container between sheets of greaseproof paper or reusable liners in the fridge for up to 1 week.

Blood orange upside-down cake

This beautiful gluten-free cake makes the most of blood oranges which are only around for a short season, but you can also use regular oranges. The almonds keep the cake moist, and the polenta gives it crunch and a chewy base. A tip for success: remember to line the tin thoroughly so that the caramel can't escape during cooking.

FEEDS 8–10

FOR THE CARAMEL
125g/4¼oz caster sugar
50ml/1¾fl oz orange juice, strained
50g/1¾oz butter

FOR THE CAKE
400g/14oz unpeeled blood oranges, washed
175g/6oz butter, softened
175g/6oz caster sugar
3 eggs, beaten
160g/5½oz fine polenta
½ tsp almond extract
2 tsp gluten-free baking powder
100g/3½oz ground almonds

1 Double-line a solid (not loose-based) 23–24cm (9–9½in) round cake tin with greaseproof paper. To make sure there are no gaps for the caramel to seep through, it is worth using two large sheets of greaseproof paper, allowing them to overlap the sides of the tin and cradle the whole cake.

2 To make the caramel, put the sugar, orange juice and 1 tablespoon of water in a small saucepan. Warm over a gentle heat, stirring, for 4–5 minutes until the sugar has dissolved, then increase the heat to medium-high and cook, without stirring this time, for another 6–8 minutes until it begins to turn a dark golden brown. Remove the pan from the heat and add the butter, taking care as it will bubble up. Stir until the butter has melted and the caramel has thickened. Pour it into the base of the lined tin and make sure it covers it entirely. Leave the caramel to set in the tin for 10 minutes.

3 Grate the zest of the oranges and set the zest aside. Thinly slice the oranges and remove the peel with scissors or a sharp knife.

4 When the caramel has set, lay the orange slices in circles on top, without overlapping them. If you have any extra slices, use them to line the sides of the cake tin.

5 Preheat the oven to 160°C fan (180°C/350°F/ Gas mark 4).

6 Beat the butter and sugar together in a bowl with a wooden spoon (or with an electric mixer) until pale and fluffy, then beat in the orange zest, eggs, polenta, almond extract and baking powder. Stir in the ground almonds. The mixture will be quite stiff.

7 Dollop the cake mixture on top of the orange slices, taking care not to dislodge the arrangement of oranges in the tin.

8 Level the top of the mixture and bake in the oven for 40–45 minutes until the cake is golden and firm – a cake tester inserted into the middle of the cake should come out clean. If there is still a significant wobble to the mixture, bake for another 5–10 minutes. Remove from the oven, place on a cooling rack and leave to cool completely in the tin.

9 To serve, place a large plate over the cake tin and turn it upside down to invert the cake onto the plate. Remove the tin, peel off the greaseproof paper, and admire your handiwork!

The cake will keep for up to 5 days in an airtight container.

Feed-a-crowd crunchy apple traybake

Few people can resist an apple cake, and when I need to feed a crowd, this is the recipe I use. It has a crunchy coconut toffee-like topping which makes a lovely contrast to the spiced apple sponge. It's a huge recipe that will happily feed lots of hungry sweet-toothed people, so don't even think about keeping it to yourself!

FEEDS 12–16

300g/10½oz caster sugar
4 eggs
220ml/7¾fl oz sunflower oil
2 tsp vanilla extract
350g/12oz plain flour
1 tsp baking powder
½ tsp bicarbonate of soda
½ tsp fine salt
2 tsp mixed spice
100g/3½oz walnuts or mixed nuts, chopped
5 eating apples, peeled, cored and
    cut into 1cm (½in) dice

FOR THE TOPPING

140g/5oz butter, plus extra for greasing
150g/5½oz soft dark brown sugar
40g/1½oz walnuts or mixed nuts, finely chopped
3 tbsp whole milk
1 tsp vanilla extract
80g/2¾oz desiccated coconut

1 Preheat the oven to 160°C fan (180°C/350°F/ Gas mark 4). Grease a large roasting or traybake tin (about 30 x 23cm/12 x 9in) with butter and line with greaseproof paper or a reusable non-stick liner.

2 To make the cake batter, beat the sugar and eggs together in a bowl with a wooden spoon (or with an electric mixer), add the oil and vanilla extract and beat until combined. Mix the dry ingredients together, then mix them into the cake batter just until you can't see any white floury streaks, then stir in the chopped nuts and apples.

3 Transfer the mixture into the tin and lightly smooth the top. Bake in the oven for 25–30 minutes until a cake tester inserted into the middle of the sponge comes out clean.

4 While the cake is baking, combine the topping ingredients in a small saucepan and heat over a medium heat until the butter has melted.

5 When the cake is ready, remove the tin from the oven. Turn off the oven and set the grill to high.

6 Pour the topping over the hot cake and smooth it evenly up to the edges of the tin.

7 Place the cake under the grill for 2–3 minutes. Watch it like a hawk as it burns very easily! As soon as it is bubbling and a light golden brown, remove and place the tin on a cooling rack.

8 Allow the cake to cool in the tin before cutting.

The cake will keep in an airtight container at room temperature for 3 days.

Carrot and raisin loaves

This is one of my favourite make-ahead cake recipes. The loaves are dark and nutty, the grated carrot keeps them moist, and they are packed with dried fruit and warm spices. The final touch is a light citrus icing. Because the loaves freeze beautifully, it would be madness not to make one for now and one for later.

MAKES 2 LOAF CAKES

280ml/9½fl oz vegetable oil
300g/10½oz soft dark brown sugar
4 eggs
2 tsp vanilla extract
grated zest and juice of 1 large washed orange
500g/1lb 2oz carrots, coarsely grated
140g/5oz raisins
50g/1¾oz hazelnuts, finely chopped
450g/1lb plain flour
¼ tsp salt
1 tsp baking powder
1 tsp bicarbonate of soda
2 tsp mixed spice
2 tsp ground cinnamon
1 tsp ground ginger

FOR THE ICING

3–4 tbsp orange juice
200g/7oz icing sugar

1 Preheat the oven to 130°C fan (150°C/300°F/ Gas mark 2) and line the base and sides of two large (900g/2lb) loaf tins with greaseproof paper or reusable non-stick liners.

2 Beat the oil and sugar together in a large mixing bowl with a wooden spoon (or with an electric mixer) until completely blended. Add the eggs one at a time, beating well after each addition, then add the vanilla extract, orange zest and 4 tablespoons of orange juice (save the rest of the juice for the icing). Stir in the grated carrot, raisins and nuts.

3 In another bowl, mix the dry loaf ingredients.

4 Add the dry ingredients to the batter a third at a time, stirring with a metal spoon between each addition. The minute you can't see any streaks of flour, stop stirring and divide the mixture equally between the two lined loaf tins.

5 Bake in the oven for 1 hour 20 minutes–1 hour 30 minutes, until a cake tester inserted into the middle of each loaf comes out clean.

6 Remove from the oven and leave to cool in the tins for 10 minutes, then transfer to a cooling rack to cool completely.

7 If you are eating the loaves immediately, mix the icing ingredients together and spread it evenly over the top.

If you are freezing the loaves, allow them to cool completely. Do not ice before freezing. Wrap tightly in foil and freeze for up to 2 months. Defrost completely and ice before serving.

Blueberry and lemon drizzle cake

This is one of my top five cakes, mostly because it's made in one bowl, it doesn't require a stand mixer or electric hand mixer, and it keeps happily for several days without drying out. Plus, the blueberries split and leak vibrant purple juices into the sponge, which looks gorgeous; and it's topped with a sour lemon drizzle, which gives it national-treasure status as far as I'm concerned. You can make this with fresh or frozen blueberries, but if you are using frozen berries, do not defrost them before using.

FEEDS 8

220g/7¾oz thick Greek yoghurt
75g/2¾oz vegetable oil
2 eggs
120g/4oz caster sugar
grated zest of 2 lemons
220g/7¾oz plain flour
1½ tsp baking powder
½ tsp bicarbonate of soda
1 tsp fine salt
150g/5½oz blueberries

FOR THE DRIZZLE
juice of 1 lemon
80g/2¾oz granulated sugar

1   Preheat the oven to 160°C fan (180°C/350°F/ Gas mark 4). Grease and line the base and sides of a 20–23cm (8–9in) round cake tin with greaseproof paper or a reusable non-stick liner.

2   Beat the yoghurt, oil, eggs, sugar and lemon zest together in a bowl.

3   Mix the flour, baking powder, bicarbonate of soda and salt together, then stir into the yoghurt mixture.

4   Gently fold in half of the blueberries and pour the mixture into the lined cake tin. Smooth the top, then scatter over the remaining blueberries.

5   Bake in the oven for 35–40 minutes, until a cake tester inserted into the middle of the cake comes out clean and the top of the cake is springy. If you are using frozen blueberries, you will need to add another 10–15 minutes to the cooking time.

6   Remove from the oven and, while it is still hot, make little holes over the top of the cake with a cake tester.

7   Mix the lemon juice and sugar and pour it over the cake while it is still hot. Smooth with a knife so that the drizzle covers the top evenly.

8   Allow to cool in the tin for 10–15 minutes then transfer to a cooling rack.

Once cooled, the cake will keep in an airtight container in the fridge for up to 3 days.

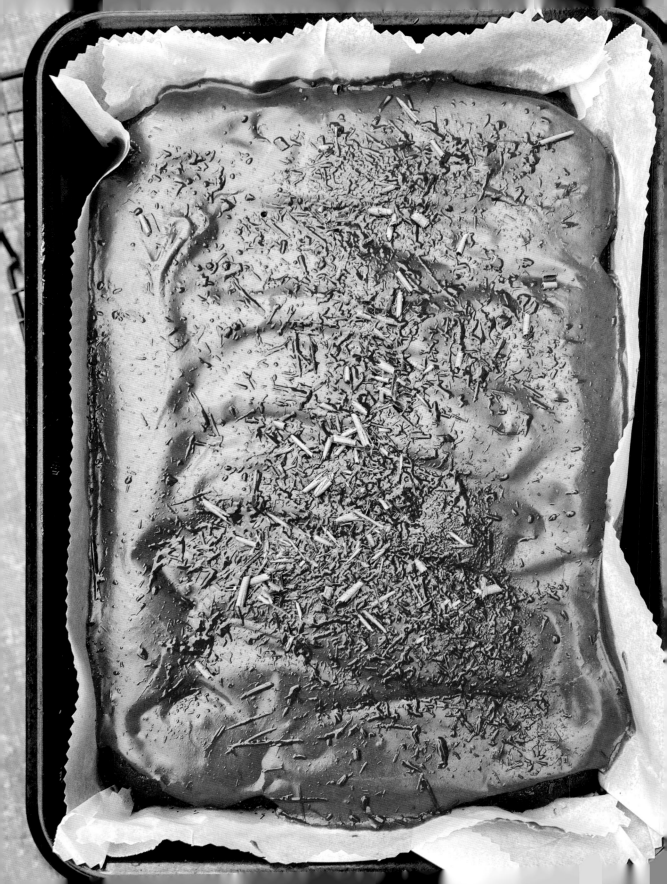

Huge chocolate and orange traybake

This gorgeous and unashamedly indulgent cake with soft, glossy icing is based on a recipe belonging to my friend Carol – it is regularly made by multiple generations of her family. If you need an insanely chocolatey cake for a birthday, a monster pudding, or the perfect 'thank you' for a group of special people, this is it. The un-iced cake can be made in advance and frozen.

FEEDS 12

125ml/4¼fl oz sunflower oil
60g/2¼oz cocoa powder
125g/4¼oz butter
250g/9oz plain flour
300g/10½oz caster sugar
pinch of salt
1 tsp bicarbonate of soda
125ml/4¼fl oz buttermilk
3 eggs, beaten
1 tsp orange extract
2 segments from a Terry's chocolate orange

FOR THE ICING

4 tbsp buttermilk
2 tbsp cocoa powder
250g/9oz icing sugar
½ tsp vanilla extract
½ tsp orange extract

1 Preheat the oven to 160°C fan (180°C/350°F/ Gas mark 4) and line a 20 x 30cm (8 x 12in) traybake tin with greaseproof paper or a reusable non-stick liner.

2 Heat 250ml/9fl oz water with the oil, cocoa powder and butter in a small saucepan and stir until the butter has melted and the ingredients are combined. Set aside to cool for a few minutes.

3 Place the flour, sugar, salt and bicarbonate of soda in a large bowl and mix well. Pour in the buttermilk, beaten eggs and orange extract and stir until combined. Add the oil and cooled cocoa mixture and mix everything together until you have a smooth batter.

4 Pour the batter into the lined tin and bake in the oven for 30–35 minutes, until a cake tester inserted into the middle of the cake comes out clean.

5 While the cake is baking, stir all the icing ingredients together in a bowl until smooth.

6 Remove the cake from the oven and let it cool in the tin for 10 minutes. Pour the icing over the top and smooth it out with a palette knife. Allow to cool completely in the tin.

7 When the cake is cool, use a potato peeler to shave curls and shards of chocolate from the chocolate orange segments. Scatter them over the top of the cake before cutting.

The cake will keep in an airtight container in the fridge for up to 5 days. To freeze the un-iced cake, allow to cool and wrap in foil or a reusable liner. Defrost and ice and decorate as above before serving.

Jumbleberry sorbet ⓥ

This unassuming sorbet packs an intense flavour and depth of colour that you wouldn't expect from such humble beginnings. It came about as a result of leftover frozen Christmas cranberries and a pack of blueberries from a short-lived smoothie obsession that were cluttering up the freezer. I turned them into this tart sorbet which is the perfect end to a rich meal. If you have an ice-cream maker and the bowl requires freezing, place it in the freezer the night before you plan to make the sorbet.

FEEDS 6

200g/7oz caster sugar
250g/9oz frozen cranberries, defrosted
250g/9oz frozen blueberries, defrosted
juice of ½ lemon
Frozen berries, to serve (optional)

1   Pour 250ml/9fl oz water into a small saucepan, add the caster sugar and stir over a low heat for 2 minutes until the sugar dissolves. Bring to the boil, reduce the heat and simmer for 3–4 minutes until the mixture thickens to a syrup. Set aside to cool.

2   Blitz the berries and lemon juice in a food processor. Strain the mixture through a sieve, pressing down on the pulp to press all the liquid through the mesh.

3   Mix the fruit juice with the sugar syrup.

4   If you have an ice-cream maker, pour in the sorbet and churn until it sets. Transfer to an airtight container and freeze. If you don't have an ice-cream maker, pour the sorbet into an airtight container, close and freeze for 2 hours. Remove and run a fork through the mixture to break up the ice crystals, then place back in the freezer for another 2 hours. Remove and fork through again and return to the freezer for another hour. Repeat twice more, or until the sorbet has set completely.

5   Remove from the freezer 10–15 minutes before serving, so it softens slightly. Optional: scatter with frozen berries to serve.

The sorbet will keep in the freezer for up to 1 month.

Cherry, coconut and banana loaf Ⓥ

This vegan loaf was created with my friend Polly, who is a brilliant baker. It's rich and sweet, packed with dark sugary tones and little treasure pockets of cherries. We often have past-their-best bananas, and when they get to the point when no one wants to eat them, I pop them in the freezer (skin on). The skins turn a not-very-fetching shade of dark brown, but they are perfect for cakes. Here they are mixed with desiccated coconut, which brings a luxuriously moist richness to what is otherwise quite a serious cake. This needs a long, slow bake but it is worth it.

MAKES 1 LARGE LOAF CAKE

3 small or 2 large ripe bananas, mashed
4 tbsp maple syrup
1 tsp vanilla extract
4 tbsp almond milk
1 flax egg*
160g/5½oz soft dark brown sugar,
    plus extra for sprinkling
1 tsp ground cinnamon
80g/2¾oz desiccated coconut
280g/10oz plain flour
1 tsp baking powder
½ tsp bicarbonate of soda
130g/4½oz vegan margarine, melted
80g/2¾oz glacé cherries, quartered

1 Preheat the oven to 160°C fan (180°C/350°F/ Gas mark 4) and line the base and sides of a large (900g/2lb) loaf tin with greaseproof paper or a reusable non-stick loaf-tin liner.

2 Beat the mashed banana, maple syrup, vanilla extract and almond milk together in a bowl until smooth. Add the flax egg and stir.

3 Mix all the dry ingredients together in a large bowl.

4 Pour the banana mixture on top of the dry ingredients, then add the melted margarine over the top. Stir the mixture just until you can't see any floury white streaks. Don't overmix as this will make the loaf too heavy.

5 Finally, add the cherries and stir until just combined. Again, don't over-stir.

6 Pour the cake batter into the prepared tin and bake for 1 hour–1 hour 10 minutes, until the top is golden brown and firm, and a cake tester inserted into the middle of the loaf comes out clean.

7 Remove from the oven and leave to cool in the tin for 10 minutes, then turn out to cool completely on a cooling rack.

The cake will keep in an airtight container at room temperature for up to 5 days.

If you are freezing the cake, allow to cool completely before freezing. Wrap tightly in foil or reusable (freezable) wrapping and freeze for up to 1 month. Defrost completely before serving.

* Mix 1 tablespoon of ground flax seed with 3 tablespoons of boiling water in a bowl. Leave to stand for 5 minutes.

Lemon and elderflower slices

Cakes made with the unique taste of fresh elderflower are sadly a short-lived seasonal treat. However, these intensely rich and lemony slices are made with elderflower cordial, which means you can enjoy its intense, heady, floral flavour all year round. This delightfully sunny and indulgent recipe looks as if it should be saved for special occasions, but it keeps well, so go ahead: make a batch and treat yourself for several days!

MAKES 20–25 SLICES

160g/5½oz butter, softened
360g/12½ oz caster sugar
grated zest and juice of 3 lemons (kept separate)
200g/7oz plain flour
1 tbsp cornflour
120ml/4fl oz single cream
5 eggs, beaten
3 tbsp elderflower cordial

1 Preheat the oven to 170°C fan (190°C/375°F/ Gas mark 5) and grease and line the base and sides of a 20cm (8in) square tin with greaseproof paper or a reusable non-stick liner.

2 Beat the butter and 100g/3½oz of the caster sugar together in a bowl with a wooden spoon (or with an electric mixer) until light and fluffy. Add a third of the lemon zest and all the plain flour and mix gently until it forms a soft dough. Do not over-mix.

3 Press the dough into the base of the lined tin and use the base of a glass or a palette knife to gently smooth the surface until it is completely flat. Prick the base all over with a fork and bake in the oven for 20–25 minutes until lightly golden. Remove from the oven and set aside to cool a little.

4 Whisk the cornflour with 1 tablespoon of the cream in a bowl, then gradually add the remaining cream, whisking as you do so to remove any lumps. Whisk in the beaten eggs a little at a time, then the remaining caster sugar and cordial.

5 Add the remaining lemon zest and all the juice to the mixture. Pour the mixture into a small saucepan and warm over a low heat for 10–12 minutes until the mixture has thickened to the consistency of lemon curd.

6 Pour the lemon mixture on top of the shortbread and bake for 15–20 minutes until it has just set and has a slight wobble when you shake the tin.

7 Remove from the oven and allow to cool completely in the tin before cutting into 20–25 slices.

The slices will keep in the fridge for up to 4 days.

Jewelled pear and ginger cake

This golden, aromatic and moist one-bowl cake is very handy for using up over-ripe pears. It takes no time to put together, but it does like a long, slow bake. It's a great recipe to take on holiday as it can be mixed by hand.

FEEDS 8

175g/6oz butter, softened, or margarine
175g/6oz caster sugar
3 eggs, beaten
3 balls of stem ginger in syrup, finely chopped
1 tbsp stem ginger syrup from the jar
175g/6oz self-raising flour
3–4 ripe pears (about 450g/1lb) peeled, cored and cut into 1cm (½in) dice
1 tbsp demerara sugar

1   Preheat the oven to 150°C fan (170°C/340°F/ Gas mark 3) and grease and line the base and sides of a 23cm (9in) round cake tin with greaseproof paper or a reusable non-stick liner.

2   Beat the butter and caster sugar together in a bowl with a wooden spoon (or with an electric mixer) until pale and fluffy.

3   Add the beaten eggs a little at a time until combined, then mix in two-thirds of the chopped ginger and all the ginger syrup. Tip in the flour and stir until you have a smooth batter, then gently fold three-quarters of the diced pear through the mixture.

4   Pour into the prepared tin and tip the remaining diced pears over the top. Level the top gently and scatter evenly with the demerara sugar. Bake in the oven for 1 hour until golden and firm to the touch – a cake tester inserted into the middle of the cake should come out clean.

5   Remove from the oven and distribute the remaining chopped ginger over the top.

6   Leave to cool in the tin for at least 20 minutes before slicing.

The cake will keep in an airtight container at room temperature for up to 4 days.

6 | Leftovers, gluts and things in jars

We all know that repurposing leftovers, finishing off the last of a jar of curry paste or finding creative ways to use up tired but edible food makes a lot of sense. It reduces waste, saves us money, and is good for the planet. In my dreams, we'd all have flocks of happy chickens who would make light work of the scraps, but that's not always an option. The reality is that, particularly when we're busy, managing the contents of our fridges and cupboards efficiently is a challenge, and no matter how good our intentions, sometimes it's just easier and faster to scrape any excess into the recycling bin or compost heap.

The answer is to have a handy list of tried-and-tested recipes in your cooking arsenal that will help you make light work of those pesky leftovers. In this chapter you'll find a few of my favourite recipes for leftovers, as well as hints and tips for dealing with seasonal gluts and some of the most commonly discarded ingredients.

But do remember, although it's good practice to make the most of what we have, there is still a limit to the delights of leftovers. I'm thinking specifically of a friend's thrifty mother who was spotted by her children emptying packets of stale crisps into a pan of vegetable soup on the grounds that they were 'still potatoes'. Needless to say, soup wasn't the most popular item on the family menu that day . . .

Things in jars

Even if you're a condiment fan, chances are you will always have a few spoonfuls left at the bottom of your jars. It probably won't be enough for a recipe, but it feels horribly wasteful to discard it. So, the jar goes back into the cupboard or fridge for a few months or weeks until it goes off, at which point you throw it out.

Luckily there are plenty of ways to use up those scraps and put them to good use before the jars make their way to the recycling bin. Just one suggestion: if you don't have one already, treat yourself to a small bendy spatula. They are invaluable for extracting every last precious molecule. Here are just a few of my favourite ways to use up those scrapes, smears and smudges.

Mustard

A smudge of mustard at the bottom of a jar is really just a salad dressing waiting to happen. Add a tablespoon of wine or cider vinegar, screw the lid on tightly and give it a good shake. Add 2 tablespoons of olive oil, some salt and pepper, and ¼ teaspoon of runny honey and shake again. Keep in the fridge for up to 3 days.

Curry and spice pastes

Even if you regularly make paste-based recipes, at some point there will not be quite enough left in the bottom of the jar for another dish. Don't throw it out. Instead, mix those smudges of leftover curry, miso, harissa or chipotle paste with a tablespoon of olive oil and toss through root vegetables before roasting.

Marmite

It's always a challenge to access every last scrap of this famous salty spread. Apparently, the answer is to lay the jar on its side, so the Marmite can helpfully migrate to one side. The downside is that it can also leak out, so I'll stick to my method: pour 3–4 tablespoons of boiling water into the jar, screw the lid on tightly and gently shake so that the Marmite dissolves. A few teaspoons of the resulting Marmite water adds a satisfyingly salty tang to soups, stews, pasta or mash.

Mincemeat

As a family, we love mince pies, but even after making big batches for Christmas we always seem to have plenty of leftover mincemeat. Every year it sat in the fridge as a sad reminder of celebrations past until our enthusiasm evaporated along with our Christmas spirit, and it was eventually thrown away. Then a thrifty friend suggested I added it to shortbread dough. These richly spiced and fruity biscuits have since become a traditional and welcome treat during January's chilly post-Christmas days.

Christmas mincemeat biscuits

These wafer-thin fruity spiced biscuits are not just melt-in-the-mouth gorgeous, they're also a brilliant freezer standby. It's a very generous recipe, so I usually freeze most of the dough in a log shape, and simply cut slices off to bake from frozen whenever there's a biscuit call.

MAKES ABOUT 60 BISCUITS

280g/10oz plain flour, plus extra for dusting
200g/7oz cold butter, cubed
140g/5oz caster sugar
1 tsp vanilla extract
1 egg
80g/2¾oz vegetarian mincemeat
4 tbsp granulated sugar

1   Place the flour and butter into a food processor and pulse until the mixture resembles fine breadcrumbs. Add the caster sugar, vanilla extract, egg and mincemeat and pulse for 2–3 seconds until you have a smooth dough, but the fruit is still visible.

2   Tip the dough out onto a floured surface and roughly shape it into a large log. Wrap the log in a sheet of cling film or reusable wrapping and gently roll until it is smooth, cylindrical and about 25cm (10in) long. Chill for 1 hour.

3   Preheat the oven to 160°C fan (180°C/350°F/ Gas mark 4) and line two baking sheets with greaseproof paper.

4   Unwrap the dough and, using a sharp knife, cut the log into about sixty 2mm (⅟₁₆in)-thick slices. Place the slices on the baking sheets.

5   Bake in the oven for 10–12 minutes until golden, then remove the baking sheets from the oven and scatter with granulated sugar. Leave to harden for 5 minutes, then transfer to a cooling rack to cool completely. The biscuits can be kept in an airtight container for up to 2 days.

The dough can be wrapped in cling film or reusable (freezable) wrapping and frozen for up to 2 months before baking. Remove from the freezer and, as soon as it is soft enough to slice, cut it into rounds and place on lined baking sheets. Bake and cool as above.

Dairy and eggs

Most dairy products will freeze quite happily, especially milk, cheese and butter, but if you're low on space in the freezer, here are a few suggestions for using up any extras.

Milk
Making sure you have enough, but not too much, milk for a busy household is virtually impossible. The reality is that you can't predict demand unless it's just you and a teapot. If you're awash with excess milk, don't jettison it down the sink, because there is a better solution. Either freeze it or use it to make a white or cheese sauce, which you can then use to make my Triple Green Lasagne (p.134) or Mushroom, Broccoli and Walnut Lasagne (p.137). You'll thank yourself when it's a lasagne kind of day and you realise that part of the recipe is already sorted.

Cheddar
There's usually no such thing as excess cheddar in our house, but if use-by dates are looming, I grate it and pop it in the freezer. It can then be added straight from the freezer to cheese sauces, bakes or toasted sandwiches.

Feta
Many feta recipes don't call for the whole pack, but it doesn't keep for long after opening. Make sure none is wasted by turning leftovers into a quick dip or sauce. Blitz the feta with a few tablespoons of chopped fresh herbs and just enough plain yoghurt to make a paste, or add more yoghurt until it is a pourable sauce. Season with salt and pepper and drizzle over roasted vegetables, or toss through warm salads.

Cheese rinds
Save cheese rinds in the fridge or freezer and add them to soups in the last 10 minutes of cooking to add cheesy richness and flavour – just remember to discard the rinds before ladling out the soup!

Yoghurt
Got some plain yoghurt left at the bottom of the carton? Mix it with curry and spice pastes or fresh herbs to make a quick salad dressing or marinade. Yoghurt can also be used in place of buttermilk in baking recipes.

Eggs
I always try to include whole eggs in my recipes, but there are times when you really do just need the yolk. Luckily, you can freeze the whites, so they don't have to go to waste. Place the egg whites in an airtight container, note the quantity on the container, and freeze. Defrost completely before using. Egg whites can be stored in the fridge for up to 2 days or frozen for up to 2 months.

It's rarer that you have extra egg yolks, but if that happens, use them to add extra richness to scrambled eggs, quiches or frittatas. Or you could try curing them. Cured egg yolk sounds like an ingredient you'd find in a Michelin-starred restaurant, but it's easy to do. The cured yolks have a rich, creamy texture and can be grated onto dishes like cheese.

Herbed, cured egg yolks

This recipe makes a batch of cured yolks infused with lemon and herbs. They will keep in the fridge in an airtight container for up to 1 month. Admittedly, it does use a lot of salt and sugar, but it is worth it! These little golden orbs are magical, infusing everything they touch with richness and flavour. Grate them over pasta, salads, toast or vegetables for a blast of umami.

MAKES 6 CURED YOLKS

350g/12oz fine salt
300g/10½oz caster sugar
finely grated zest of 1 lemon
½ tbsp finely chopped rosemary leaves
½ tbsp finely chopped thyme leaves
6 eggs

1 In a small bowl, mix the salt, sugar, lemon zest and the chopped rosemary and thyme leaves.

2 Tip half the salt mixture into a small plastic container or tray in which the egg yolks will fit without touching.

3   Separate the egg yolks from the whites. The egg whites can be stored in the fridge for up to 2 days or frozen for up to 2 months and used for other recipes.

4   Make 6 small, yolk-shaped indentations in the salt mix with a spoon. Gently place the yolks in the indentations, making sure they don't touch, and scatter over the remaining salt mixture so that they are completely covered.

5   Cover the container or tray and place it in the fridge for 4 days. Check the yolks and if they feel firm, they are ready. If they still feel slightly liquid, return to the fridge for another 2 days.

6   When the yolks are ready, brush off the salt mixture and rinse gently. Pat them dry.

7   Heat the oven to its lowest setting and lightly grease a metal cooling rack. Place the yolks on the rack in the oven for 1 hour, until they are dry.

8   Cool completely and keep in an airtight container in the fridge for up to 1 month.

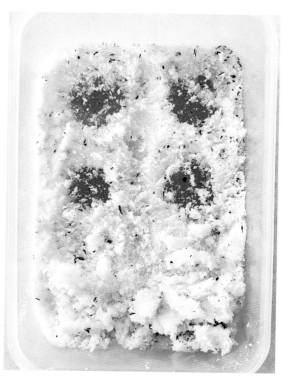

LEFTOVERS, GLUTS AND THINGS IN JARS **211**

Fresh fruit and veg

Even if you're a super-organised shopper, it's probably still mostly fruit and vegetables that end up in your bin or food recycling. There are always bits and pieces that can't be salvaged, but the ideas below will help to make the most of a few of our most frequently wasted purchases. And, of course, if you can use seasonal bounty to create useful content for your empty jars and bottles, so much the better.

Herbs

Rosemary and thyme are robust, woody herbs which freeze well, as do finely chopped fresh chilli, garlic and ginger. Soft herbs such as parsley, chives and coriander become soggy when they defrost, so they aren't good for garnishing, but you can still freeze them and use them to add to recipes during cooking. Mint can be frozen in ice cubes and added to your favourite summer cocktails and mocktails.

Sad tomatoes

If your fresh tomatoes have lost their mojo, turn them into frozen flavour bombs. Place 2 tablespoons of olive oil and a chopped garlic clove into a small pan over a medium heat. Cook for 2 minutes, then add 400g/14oz roughly chopped tomatoes and cook for 10 minutes. Season to taste, cool and freeze. Defrost when needed and add to pasta sauces, soups and stews.

Salad leaf pesto

Wilting salad leaves or unfinished bags of greenery such as rocket, watercress or pea shoots can be turned into instant pesto. Blitz the leaves for a few seconds in a processor with fresh garlic, grated cheese (or a vegan alternative) and enough olive oil to give it a smooth dropping consistency. Add almonds, peanuts or hazelnuts and process briefly. Drizzle a little olive oil over the top of the pesto to help preserve the colour. Store in a sealed container in the fridge for up to 3 days.

Apples and pears

Fruit is a gift for the frugal baker. Apples and pears just past their best work brilliantly in cakes, adding a dense moistness to bouncy sponges that can also double up as puddings. The trick is to cook the cakes long and slow and allow them time to firm up before serving. Stewed or puréed apples and pears also freeze well. I always use a family recipe for this which is super easy: peel, core and chop the fruit into small chunks and place in a small saucepan. Add 1 teaspoon of caster sugar, ½ teaspoon of lemon juice and 1 teaspoon of water per piece of fruit. Add an optional pinch of cinnamon. Cook for 8–10 minutes until the fruit has softened but still holds its shape. Allow to cool completely before storing in the fridge for up to 2 days or the freezer for up to 1 month.

Peaches, plums and nectarines

These smooth-skinned fruits come in warm colours and are most beguiling during the summer months, but they don't last long and as soon as the wrinkles set in, they become less appealing. That's when it's time to make tarts. Stone and slice the fruit thinly, and place on a sheet of puff pastry. Sprinkle with sugar, bake in the oven until golden, and pretend you've just collected the tarts from a French patisserie. You can also use any unwanted fruit to make simple fruit compotes for the freezer.

Berries

Liven up your uneaten berries or hedgerow gluts by making a bottle of homemade berry-flavoured gin. Blackberry gin has a wonderful deep purple hue and an intense blackberry flavour. If you are lucky enough to have very productive brambles nearby, make a few extra bottles for Christmas presents.

Bay and blackberry gin Ⓥ

The intense flavour and colour of this gin is best in the first month after opening, but it will keep for up to 1 year.

MAKES 2 SMALL (APPROX. 350ML/12FL OZ) BOTTLES

350g/12oz blackberries
150g/5½oz caster sugar
700ml/24fl oz gin
2 bay leaves

1 Wash and sterilise a large jar with a capacity of 1 litre/34fl oz, or two smaller jars.

2 Place the berries and sugar in the bottom of the jar(s). Pour in the gin and bay leaves and stir. Seal the jar(s) and place in a cool, dark place for 3 weeks. Each day, shake the jar(s) to help the sugar to dissolve, then place back in the dark.

3 After 3 weeks, open the jar(s) and strain the gin through a muslin cloth or a paper coffee filter into sterilised bottles. Seal the bottles. After opening, consume within 1 month.

For adding an extra kick to cocktails, place the drained blackberries on a baking tray and open-freeze for 1–2 hours. When they are firm, pop them into an airtight bag or box and freeze. The frozen berries can be added to cocktails or prosecco.

Storecupboard

Storecupboard ingredients can be sneaky little things. Because they don't live in the fridge, you can be fooled into thinking they will last for ever. But, as with many foodstuffs, their long-life credentials last only until they are opened, then all bets are off.

Nuts

Nuts have a shorter shelf life than you'd think, which is a shame because many recipes only use a few handfuls. Either make several batches of the recipe or lightly toast any extra nuts and use them to add extra texture and crunch to salads and stir fries or add to granolas or crumble mixtures.

Dried fruit

Christmas and fruit cake recipes traditionally rely on many different dried fruits and peel to get a good balance of flavours and sweetness. But it also means they will often only use a small quantity of each one. Chop up the lonely leftovers and add them to couscous and salads, curries, stews and fried rice.

Preserves

Small amounts of your favourite preserves can be just what a recipe needs to reach peak perfection. Try adding your last tablespoon of marmalade to a chocolate cake mixture to give it a subtle orange flavour, or swirl a little hot water around almost-empty jars of pip-free berry preserves and then add to gravies and sauces.

Antipasti

What can you do with just a few olives, sun-dried tomatoes, artichokes or peppers in oil? Well, quite a lot really. Chop them finely, season with salt and pepper and toss them, along with any oil left in the jar, with hot pasta, cooked rice or grains. Chopped olives, sun-dried tomatoes and peppers also make a great dip or toast topping when mixed with cream cheese (or a vegan alternative).

Pesto

On the rare occasions when we have a spoonful or two of pesto leftover, it usually goes straight on top of a jacket potato, but another clever way to stretch and use up this luscious paste is to mix it with 1–2 tablespoons of olive oil and drizzle it over your favourite pizza or roasted vegetables.

Easter eggs

If you have young children or a sweet tooth, you will probably have found yourself awash with Easter eggs at some point. They are usually made of super-sweet chocolate, and you might not want the kids (or yourself) to eat them all at once. A good way of ensuring a more balanced supply of chocolate is to divert some towards a big batch of chocolate chip cookie dough. You can freeze it in cookie-sized portions, ready to place in the oven when Easter is a distant memory and there is an urgent need for chocolate.

Easter egg chocolate chip cookies

This recipe makes enough cookie dough for two big batches so you can freeze half if you aren't feeding a crowd. The recipe can also be halved.

MAKES 40 LARGE, CHEWY, AND DELIRIOUSLY GOOD COOKIES

250g/9oz butter, softened
250g/9oz caster sugar
250g/9oz soft dark brown sugar
2 tsp vanilla extract
2 eggs, beaten
450g/1lb plain flour
1 tsp baking powder
280g/10oz chocolate Easter eggs,
    roughly chopped

1   Preheat the oven to 170°C fan (190°C/375°F/ Gas mark 5) and line two large baking sheets with greaseproof paper.

2   Beat the butter and caster sugar together in a bowl with a wooden spoon (or with an electric mixer) until pale and fluffy, then gradually beat in the brown sugar. Add the vanilla extract and eggs and beat until combined.

3   Combine the flour and baking powder then add them to the butter, sugar and egg mixture and mix until you have a soft and sticky dough. Stir the chopped Easter eggs evenly through the dough.

4   Scoop generously heaped tablespoons of the mixture onto the baking sheets, leaving 3–4cm (1¼–1½in) between each one.

5   Bake in the oven for 15–18 minutes until golden around the edges, but still pale in the middle. Remove from the oven and leave to cool on the baking sheets for 10 minutes before transferring them to a cooling rack to cool completely.

To freeze the cookies before baking, place the baking sheets of unbaked cookie dough in the freezer for 30 minutes to open-freeze. As soon as they are firm, tip them into an airtight bag and freeze for up to 2 months. Cook from frozen as above, for 18–20 minutes.

Index